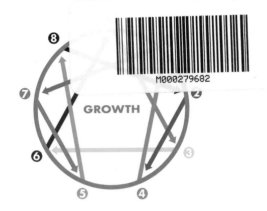

GROWTH

1 — GOODNESS · TRUTH · PERFECTION · CLARITY · JUSTICE · SELF CONTROL

2 — HELPFULNESS · ALTRUISM · LOVING · BOLD · SERVANTS HEART · DISCERNING NEEDS

3 — EFFICIENCY · ACTION · ENCOURAGER · ESTABLISHER · INSPIRING · EXCELLENCE

4 — CREATIVITY · EMPATHY · LOVE OF BEAUTY · SPACE SAVER · EMOTIONALLY HONEST

5 — WISDOM · VISION · STEADFASTNESS · CLARITY · FAITHFULNESS · HUMILITY

6 — COURAGE · GUARDIANSHIP · KINDNESS · LOYALTY · STRENGTH · FAITHFULNESS

7 — SPONTANEITY · JOY · THANKFULNESS · HOPE · LONG SUFFERING · VISION

8 — STRENGTH · ZEAL · VIGILANT · JUSTICE · PROTECTOR · TENDERNESS

9 — UNDERSTANDING · PEACE · KINDNESS · EMPATHY · PATIENCE · GENTLENESS

WHAT PEOPLE ARE SAYING ABOUT ELISABETH BENNETT AND *THE THINKER: GROWING AS AN ENNEAGRAM 5*

As an Enneagram Five who loves to research why I love to research, I have found this book to be a necessary and vital part of my library. Reading *The Thinker* has both encouraged and challenged me to see my strengths and weaknesses clearly while paying close attention to how God may use them to draw me closer to Himself. Elisabeth Bennett has done the incredible with this one—she's encapsulated what it means to be a Five, and how to use the undying quest for knowledge in a healthy and life-giving way to serve God. I highly recommend this for anyone who may themselves be a Five, or loves someone who is. The clarity and insight gained is well worth your time.

—*Jen Babakhan*
Author, *Detoured: The Messy, Grace-Filled Journey From Working Professional to Stay-at-Home Mom*

Elisabeth has written a delightful devotional full of important information for those who want to grow in their own self-awareness and relationship with Christ. I highly recommend reading this book so you can experience transformation on a much deeper level that will bring about the change you desire in life.

—*Beth McCord*
YourEnneagramCoach.com
Author of 10 Enneagram books

Elisabeth has a beautiful way of guiding the reader into a deeper understanding and self-awareness that leads to spiritual growth through the Enneagram. Through biblically sound and practical devotions, she helps you move from, "Okay, I know what type I am but what's next?" to personal, relational, and spiritual growth, so that you can live in the fullness of who you were created to be in your unique type.

—*Justin Boggs*
The Other Half Podcast
Enneagram coach, speaker, entrepreneur

Through her beautifully articulate words, Elisabeth accurately portrays the shadow side of each Enneagram type while also highlighting the rich grace and freedom found in the spiritual journey of integration. Pairing Scripture with reflection questions and prayers, the devotions help guide the reader on the pathway of personal and spiritual growth in a powerful way that is unique to their type.

—*Meredith Boggs*
The Other Half Podcast

If you know your Enneagram type and you're ready to make meaningful steps toward growth, this book is for you. Elisabeth combines her Enneagram expertise with her deep faith to guide readers toward self-understanding, growth, and transformation through contemplative yet practical writing. This devotional is a great tool that you'll return to again and again.

—*Steph Barron Hall*
Nine Types Co.

60-DAY ENNEAGRAM DEVOTIONAL

the
THINKER

GROWING AS AN ENNEAGRAM

ELISABETH BENNETT

WHITAKER
HOUSE

Introduction images created by Katherine Waddell.
Photo of Elisabeth Bennett by Jena Stagner of One Beautiful Life Photography.

THE THINKER
Growing as an Enneagram 5

www.elisabethbennettenneagram.com
Instagram: @enneagram.life
Facebook.com/enneagramlife

ISBN: 978-1-64123-572-3
eBook ISBN: 978-1-64123-573-0
Printed in the United States of America
© 2021 by Elisabeth Bennett

Whitaker House
1030 Hunt Valley Circle
New Kensington, PA 15068
www.whitakerhouse.com

Library of Congress Control Number: 2021941417

1 2 3 4 5 6 7 8 9 10 11 **Ⱳ** 28 27 26 25 24 23 22 21

DEDICATION

*To all the Fives holding this devotional,
you have everything you need because you have Christ.*

Contents

FOREWORD

I was in the fourth grade when I became an expert on the blue whale. I knew everything there was to know about the largest animal on earth. (Some things you just can't forget, regardless of how much time has passed.) By default, that meant my parents did too. I would ask random questions such as, "Mom, did you know the blue whale uses baleen to sift through the water and retain the four tons of krill it eats?" My parents pretended to be in awe of my borderline useless facts, like any good parents of a curious and always learning Enneagram Five.

At the time, I had no idea what the Enneagram was; I just knew I loved to learn. In fourth grade, my expertise was the blue whale; in fifth grade, it was the Great Quake of 1906, which also led to an intense fear of earthquakes for a bit, since we lived in California. No matter what caught my attention, I read all I could, storing facts like a squirrel hoarding acorns for winter. Why was it I felt better—somehow *safer*—if I knew more?

I've lived with anxiety humming steadily in the background of my life for as long as I can remember. Without being conscious of the reason, I've often turned to research to quiet it. I know, Google is *not* really my friend. To an Enneagram Five, though, Google is the best frenemy there ever was. Endless information at our fingertips—what could be bad about that? We Fives operate under a mistaken belief that the answers to everything exist somewhere, most likely just outside of our always-reaching grasp. We believe the lie, *If I know enough, I can solve any problem.*

When my mom was diagnosed with stage four cancer in 2017, my *research will fix this* belief kicked into overdrive. I pored over the latest studies and data for hours, searching for anything that would relieve my pain of knowing, deep down, that her healing was out of my hands. Her cure, which ultimately arrived in heaven, was up to God. It was the kind of reality check that a Five hates. For us Fives, faith is the opposite of our nature, which seeks certainty and feeling competent. If we don't *know* for a fact, then what do we do? Can we research our way to knowing the unknowable things of God?

Maybe your insatiable desire to learn more, to *know* more, has brought you to this book. You want to learn about why you love to learn and how to reconcile your not-so-great and sometimes super-annoying tendency to have to get to the bottom of it all. And that's the problem, isn't it? There's no *getting to the bottom* of God. He's endless.

We hate to admit it, but faith sometimes brings more questions than answers. Rest assured, we just have to know one answer: Jesus. He is *the* answer, the one that our hearts most long to find. All of the searching and wondering is exhausting, isn't it? When we can settle into the truth that He is the only answer we need, we find rest—not the kind of rest that lasts for a moment before we pick up our phones again, but real rest, the kind that makes our souls sigh in relief. It is then we can lay our need to know it all at the feet of the One who truly does know it all.

For the next sixty days, you'll take a beautiful journey that is yours and God's alone. In this moment, you are accepting an invitation to truly discover all that God has created you to be in

Christ. What does the work of God look like through you and the way He uniquely created you?

I'm so excited for all of the ways God will use *The Thinker* in your life. There is much to learn in these pages. I invite you to dig in deep, seek what Jesus has for you—inquisitive and curious *you*—and grow closer to the One who loves you best.

—Jen Babakhan
Author, *Detoured: The Messy, Grace-Filled Journey From Working Professional to Stay-at-Home Mom*

ACKNOWLEDGMENTS

My journey from young hopeful writer, all the way back to the tender age of four, to holding books with my name on them hasn't been easy or pretty. In fact, it's held a lot of hurt, disappointment, and rejection. However, as you hold a book with my name on the cover in your hands, I'd love you to know who and what has sustained me through it all. You are holding a piece of God's redemption in my story, tangible proof of His kindness, and testament of His faithfulness. I didn't break any doors down or *do* anything myself that ensured my trajectory of publishing. God in His kindness handed me this opportunity, and to Him alone belongs all the glory and praise.

My agent Amanda deserves the highest of thanks and admiration. Thank you for answering my many questions, guiding, and giving me the confidence to do this. I couldn't have done it without you. To all the people at Whitaker House, my editor Peg and publisher Christine, thank you for making these devotionals what they are today. It's been a pleasure working with you all.

To my writing community hope*writers, thank you for giving me the courage to call myself a writer long before I felt like one. To Jen Babakhan, thank for being such a great public example of Five-ness and being so generous with your gifts. I'm so grateful you wrote the foreword for this devotional.

Thank you to Pastor Bubba Jennings at Resurrection Church for reading over my proposal and giving me advice on how to serve Jesus well in this process.

The people who have been the biggest support and help to me during this process and, if I'm honest, my life, are:

Dad (Joe Upton), thank you for being one of the first people to read this devotional and for being a strong and loving presence in my life. I appreciate you more than you know! Thank you for your steadiness, faithfulness, and how you love us.

Jarrett Bradley, I am just so thrilled you wrote for this devotional! I think you were the first person I knew was a Five after being introduced to the Enneagram, and you have been such a great representation of the Five's strengths in my mind. Thank you for stepping outside your comfort zone and being generous with your words in this book.

Anna Yates, thank you for serving so faithfully as our moderator on @5ish_andiknowit. Your wisdom, passion, and steadiness are admirable, and I loved learning more about you through what you wrote for your fellow Fives in this book. You're truly a treasure! Thank you.

To all the other Fives who have left a big impact on me: Myquillyn Smith, Sara Dixon, Jasmine Holmes, all my Enneagram Five clients, and a couple of other suspected Fives whom I won't publicly "type" here. Thank you!

For all the figures in my childhood who greatly encouraged my Five-wing: Miss Frizzle (*The Magic School Bus*), Bill Nye the Science Guy, Fred Rogers, Steve Irwin, Alex Trebek, David Attenborough (*Planet Earth* narrator), Frank Peretti, Mr. Whittaker (*Adventures in Odyssey*), George Lucas, all the people on *MythBusters*, the History Channel, and the Pleasant Company. Thank you for teaching me so much!

John and Jan Bennett, thank you for faithfully praying for me and supporting me through this entire process. Your encouragement has moved mountains and sustained me on the hardest days.

Mom and Dad (Joe and Diane Upton), thank you for literally teaching me to read and write and encouraging me to say yes to big things. I would never have had the foundation to say yes without you and how you raised me. I'm so proud and grateful to have the two of you in my corner cheering me on.

Sarah and Jan, thank you for being Wellington's playmates for four hours every week so I could write. These books, more than anything, were made possible by you!

Peter, you've been beyond supporting, patient, and caring toward me. I don't know what else I would've expected from a One. You have taught me so much about what it means to be faithful, and you never let me quit. You believe in me enough for both of us, and I can't believe the gift that you are in my life. You're my best friend, and I love you.

INTRODUCTION
What Is the Enneagram?

The Enneagram is an ancient personality typology for which no one really knows the origins.

It uses nine points within a circle—the word itself means "a drawing of nine"—to represent nine distinct personality types. The points are numbered simply to differentiate between them, with each point having no greater or less value than the others. The theory is that a person assumes one of these personalities in childhood as a reaction to discovering that the world is a scary, unkind place that is unlikely to accept their true self.

The nine types are identified by their numbers or by these names:

1. The Perfectionist
2. The Helper
3. The Achiever
4. The Individualist
5. The Thinker
6. The Guardian
7. The Enthusiast
8. The Challenger
9. The Peacemaker

HOW DO I FIND MY TYPE?

Your Enneagram type is determined by your main motivation. Finding your Enneagram type is a journey, as we are typically unaware of our motivations and instead focus on our behaviors. Many online tests focus on behaviors, and while some motivations *may* produce certain behaviors, this may not always be the case, and you are unlikely to get accurate results.

To find your Enneagram type, you need to start by learning about *all* nine Enneagram types—and exploring their motivations in contrast to your own behaviors and deeper motivations.

You can ask for feedback from those around you, but most often, the more you learn, the clearer your core number shines through.

It's often the number whose description makes you feel the most *exposed* that is your true core type. Your core Enneagram number won't change, since it's solidified in childhood.

Each number's distinct motivation:

1. Integrity – Goodness
2. Love – Relationships
3. Worth – Self-Importance
4. Authenticity – Unique Identity
5. Competency – Objective Truth
6. Security – Guidance
7. Satisfaction – Freedom
8. Independence – Control
9. Peace – Equilibrium

IS THIS JOURNEY WORTH IT?

Yes! The self-awareness you gain along the way is gold, and learning about the other types in the process brings you so much empathy and understanding for all of the other personalities in your life.

WHAT MAKES THE ENNEAGRAM UNIQUE AND DIFFERENT FROM MYERS-BRIGGS, STRENGTHSFINDER, OR DISC ASSESSMENTS?

The Enneagram, unlike other typology systems, is fluid. Yes, the Enneagram tells you what your base personality characteristics are, but it also reveals how you change when you're growing, stressed, secure, unhealthy, healthy, etc.

You are not the same person at twenty as you are at sixty. You're not the same person at your stressful workplace as you are when binge-watching your favorite TV show and eating ice cream at home. The Enneagram accounts for these inconsistencies and changes in your behavior and informs you of when or how those changes occur.

If you look at the following graph, you'll see that each of the numbers connects to two other numbers by arrows. The arrow pointed toward your number is your growth arrow; the arrow pointed away is your stress number. When your life leaves you with more room to breathe, you exhibit positive characteristics of your growth number, and when you're stretched thin in seasons of stress, you exhibit the negative characteristics of your stress number.

This is one explanation for big shifts in personality over a lifetime.

Another point of difference between the Enneagram and other typology systems is *wings*. Your wings are the two numbers on either side of your core number, which add flavor to your per-

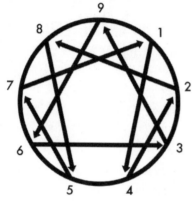

sonality type. Although your core number won't change—and your main motivation, sin proclivities, and personality will come from that core number—your wings can be very influential on your overall personality and how it presents itself. There are many different theories about wings, but the viewpoint we hold to is:

◆ Your wing can only be one of the two numbers on either side of your core number. Therefore, you can be a 5 with a 6 wing (5w6) but not a 5 with a 7 wing (5w7).

◆ You have access to the numbers on either side of your number, but most people will only have one dominant wing. (*Dominant* meaning you exhibit more of the behaviors of one wing than the other wing.) It is possible to have equal wings or no wing at all, but this is rare.

◆ Your dominant wing number can change from one to the other throughout your life, but it's speculated this might only happen once.

As you read through this book, we will go over what an Enneagram Five looks like with both of its wings. If you're struggling to figure out what your core number is, this book series could really help give you some more in-depth options!

HOW DO YOU BECOME YOUR TYPE?

Personality is a kind of shield we pick up and hide behind. It is functional, even protective at times, but altogether unnecessary because God made us in His image from the start. However, we cling to this personality like it's our key to survival, and nothing has proven us wrong so far. It's the only tool we've ever had, and the shield has scratches and dents to prove its worth.

Not all parts of our personality are wrong or bad, but by living in a fallen, sinful world, we all tend to distort even good things in bad ways. Amen?

What personality did you pick up in childhood? If you're reading this devotional, then you may have chosen type Five. Your need to be competent became the one thing that your life would rotate around from early in childhood up until right now, at this very moment.

The Enneagram talks about childhood wounds and how we pick a particular shield as a reaction to these wounds. However, not all siblings have the same Enneagram type even though they heard the same wounding message or had the same harmful experiences growing up. This is because we are born with our own unique outlook on the world, and we filter everything through that outlook. You and your siblings may have heard the same things, but while you heard, "It is not okay to be comfortable in the world," your sister heard, "You're only loved when you're successful." Thus, you both would become different Enneagram types.

Trauma and abuse of all kinds can definitely impact your choice of shield as well. If you think of all these nine shields as being a different color, perhaps you were born predisposed to be more likely to pick blue than red. However, in a moment of early trauma, you might have heard someone shouting, "Pick black! Black is the only option!" Thus, you chose black instead of blue, which would've been your own unique reaction to your life circumstances. It's hard to say how these things happen exactly, especially when trauma is involved. Are you who you are *despite* trauma...or because of it? Only God knows, but there is healing and growth to be found either way.

We've all heard the phrase, "You can't teach an old dog new tricks." I'd like to propose that when referencing personality, it might be said, "The longer you use your personality, the harder it is to see its ineffectiveness." It's not impossible for an older person to drastically change for the better, but it will be harder for them to put down what has worked for them for so long. That's why, as we age, it can become harder to even see where our personality ends and our true self begins. Even if the unhealthy parts of our personality have been ineffective, they still seem to be the only things that have worked for us.

WHY DO WE NEED THE ENNEAGRAM WHEN WE HAVE THE HOLY SPIRIT AND THE BIBLE TO GUIDE US?

The Enneagram is a helpful tool, but only when it is used as such. The Enneagram cannot save you—only Jesus can do that.

However, God made us all unique, and we all reflect Him in individual ways. Learning about these unique reflections can encourage us, as well as point us toward our purposes. The Enneagram also reveals the sin problems and blind spots of each type with which you may unknowingly struggle. Revealing these can lead us to repentance and change before God.

HOW DO I CHANGE MY MORE NEGATIVE BEHAVIORS?

Alcoholics Anonymous was really on to something when they called their first step "admitting you have a problem." How do you solve a problem if you don't know you have one or are in denial about it? You can't. If you have a shield you're using to protect yourself from the world, but are blissfully unaware of its existence, you won't understand how its very existence impacts you and your relationships. You definitely won't be putting that battered but battle-tested shield of a personality down anytime soon.

Similar to the wisdom of admitting one has a problem before recovery can begin, the Enneagram proposes self-knowledge as the starting point before there can be change.

Whether you're 100 percent sure you are an Enneagram Five, or just curious about the possibility, this is what it looks like to be a Five.

WHAT IT MEANS TO BE A THINKER

Enneagram Fives are known as the Investigator or the Thinker because of their rich thought life and position as a perpetual learner. Fives can be introverted to their very core, hoarding what little energy they have like Smaug's treasure. They are the least outwardly emotional number on the Enneagram and collect a wealth of knowledge when they are interested in a topic. They are not easily offended, are calm in a crisis, and spend a lot of time thinking, hence the name the Thinker.

Growing up, Sara lived in a small town, so her parents would do all of their big errands that required them going to a big city in one day. She remembers that, when she was around five years old, she would look forward to the big shopping day, but by lunchtime, she was a wreck: tired and grumpy. She just couldn't be out in the world anymore and was ready to go home.

Sara doesn't remember a time when she wasn't nagged by the feeling of *I just want to go home*. As Sara grew up, she adapted and would bring a book so she could stay in the car during errands, but this, among other encounters, made her feel different and misunderstood.

Sara had an active social life and lots of friends in high school, but she still felt unknown, like an outsider. She didn't know how to share her inner world with anyone and wasn't sure anyone was even interested. Even now, she knows she is loved and cared for but often feels like nobody really knows her true self.

Sara is an Enneagram Five, the Thinker, and coming to understand this about herself has given her so much insight and appreciation into why she is the way she is. She can now see her objectivity and calmness in crisis as a gift, and she works to help those around her understand what she is thinking and feeling.

A healthy Five not only understands and observes the world but enriches others with their wisdom. A healthy Five might still feel the inner panic of the world pulling on their resources, but no longer gives in to its demands as much as is instinctual. Healthy Fives prioritize the relationships that are important to them by openly communicating their needs and boundaries. These Fives will be masters in whatever "topic" piques their interest, and they often write books and teach.

An average slightly unhealthy Five will need a lot of time to process and think things through before acting, and may experience a fair amount of social anxiety. An average Five won't view themselves as isolated, but will rarely accept a spontaneous invitation and tend to hoard their energy. Feeling the need to have strong personal opinions can lead average Fives into being unintentionally argumentative and negative. Sensing others don't put the same amount of thought as they do into any given subject, an average Five will often come off as arrogant.

When reading anything about very unhealthy Fives, I can't help but picture Ted Kaczynski, the Unabomber, because an unhealthy Five will often become a textbook recluse. With only themselves to fact check their thought life, they often fall prey to odd or extreme ideals. They'll demonize social structures and purposely push people away by being rude and argumentative.

Fives have a rich inner world and often retreat from everyone and everything else to rest and replenish in the world they've created in their head. Fives struggle with the unknown and try to fix any doubts they have with knowledge.

ALL ABOUT BEING A FIVE

MOTIVATION

To Be Competent

Fives desire to know what is unknown, and be respected as competent.

BIGGEST FEAR

Being Incompetent

Fives' biggest fear is being incompetent, useless, helpless, lacking, and undeserving of others' respect or relationship.

HEAD TRIAD

Each Enneagram type is dominant in either feeling, thinking, or doing. These *triads* are referred to as heart-centered, head-centered, and gut-centered.

Fives, along with Sixes and Sevens, are considered to be part of the head triad. This means that they receive all information as something that needs to be thought over and analyzed before they can trust their feelings or gut with processing it. Analysis paralysis, dread, mental exhaustion, and anxiety are some things that this triad can struggle with as they experience the world *head first*. This is the most pronounced in Sixes as they take information in as something to analyze and then analyze their own conclusion. In comparison, Sevens tend to move on quickly to emotion: "How does this information make me feel?" And Fives move on quickly to action: "How does this information impact what I do?"

CHILDHOOD WOUND

The wounding message a Five child heard (or thought they heard) was, "It is not okay to be comfortable in the world," or "You don't have enough (fill in the blank) to make it here." The reality of how much the world would ask of the Five—emotionally, physically, and mentally—was made very clear to them as children who had either withdrawn or over-involved parents, either of which can cause a Five child to build walls around themselves and retreat into their minds.

A Five could've heard this message when their parents or guardian consistently required more of them than the Five had the energy for. The Five might have heard, "I'm just helping you prepare for real life," or "You're going to have to go places and socialize when you're an adult," or "You want to do that?" Perhaps the parent or guardian said, "You're just not smart (or athletic) enough to do that," or "You can't stay at home," or "You're just being lazy," or "The world doesn't revolve around you."

THE LOST CHILDHOOD MESSAGE FIVES LONG TO HEAR

"Your Needs Are Not a Problem"

If, as a child, a Five could have been confident that their needs would be met, they wouldn't have to hoard resources or feel like they are on their own to "make it." Jesus tells us in Matthew 6: 25–34 not to be anxious about our lives but to rest in His care for us. When you have Jesus, you don't have to worry about "being enough" because you're not left to your own devices and you have nothing to prove.

DEFENSE MECHANISM

Isolation

Isolation is the defensive mechanism most used by Fives. Fives isolate to protect themselves and their energy stores from the world. They do this by retreating into their mind—which can be an everyday occurrence—or, less often, by separating themselves physically from others.

Fives also isolate by separating their thoughts from their feelings and their feelings from their actions. They isolate their work life from their personal life, and family relationships from their other relationships.

WINGS

A wing is one of the numbers on either side of your Enneagram number that adds some *flavor* to your type. You'll still be your core number in essence, but your wing can impact a lot of your behaviors.

Five with a Four Wing (5w4)

Emotion and knowledge go to war in the mind of a Five with a Four wing. Usually uniquely quiet, interesting, creatively driven, and deep thinkers, these Fives have the best and worst of both worlds. Being a logical thinker and yet having emotions that aren't logical can make a 5w4 feel unbalanced. However, having those two sides gives them so much insight into the world of both thinking and emotional types. This is why they can offer objective, empathetic advice, and many such Fives enjoy work in careers that utilize this strength. The emotional part of a Four is usually very private for a 5w4, and although you might see a glimpse of their emotional depth in a group setting, they often process their tears and anxiety in private. The tension in this type is uniquely difficult as this wing type crosses the existential divide at the bottom of the Enneagram between heart and head.

Five with a Six Wing (5w6)

Fives with a Six wing are more social than other fives, but they still have lots of anxiety surrounding their energy stores. The loyalty aspect of Sixes puts a unique flavor on an otherwise "happy to be alone" Five. This makes them great long-distance and once-in-a-blue-moon friends. They won't question your friendship even when time, distance, or lack of communication might make you think otherwise. More in their heads than Sixes, a Five with a Six wing will often calm their anxious mind with knowledge. This type struggles with the tension between loyalty and having a low battery life. Despite this, the 5w6 is always there for their most loyal few.

ARROWS

The arrows are the two numbers your Enneagram number is connected to in the Enneagram diagram. These two arrows represent the number from which you get the best traits as you grow or the number from which you get the worst traits when you're in seasons of stress.

Stress: Going to Seven

In stress, a normally organized and thoughtful Five will start to behave like an unhealthy Seven. Scattered, noncommittal, and even hyperactive, a stressed-out Five can be easy to spot.

Growth: Going to Eight

In growth, a Five will start picking up the healthy behaviors of Eights. Normally detached and withdrawn, a secure Five will become more assertive, social, and decisive like an Eight.

TYPE FIVE SUBTYPES

When we talk about subtypes and the Enneagram, we are referring to three relational instincts we all have. These instincts, like those of *fight or flight*, are reactions over which we have little control. The three relational subtypes are Self-Preservation (Sp), Social (So), and One-to-One (Sx). We all have the capacity to use all three of these instincts, but one of them is usually dominant. That dominant subtype can strongly impact how your distinct Enneagram type looks to the rest of us.

The "Battery Life" Five (Sp)

Self-Preservation Fives are very aware of their own boundaries and aren't shy about asking for space, making them the most obvious Five. Since they don't often overdo it and are professionals at saving energy, they can actually be very happy or talkative in the social situations they do end up attending. Illness and physical struggles really impact this subtype, and an illness can actually cause this Five to dip into depression.

The "Tribe" Five (So)

Social subtype Fives dive feet-first into topics of interest and often want to unload or teach others about what they're learning. They love finding groups of people who are interested in the same thing they are and become very loyal to their "tribe." No matter how close they are to others, they always maintain some anonymity.

Within this subtype, a Four wing will cause a lot of tension between the Five's need for independence or ambiguity and their wing's need for closeness and being understood. If Fives with a Four wing feel like they have overshared in an effort to achieve closeness, they can experience a "vulnerability hangover." On the other hand, a Six wing can make this subtype more dutiful or definitive in their thinking, which is why this subtype can mistype as a One.

The Faithful Five (Sx)

One-to-one instinct Fives will still appear very reserved on the outside, only letting one or two people truly see their depth and passion. These Fives have strong connections with only a few people and are fully satisfied in those relationships. However, they can become very possessive of those few relationships, wanting the same kind of exclusivity in return, so that *their* person won't be wooed away. It can be common for this Five to mistype as either of their wing numbers or even as a very quiet Eight.

SO I'M A FIVE. WHAT NOW?

Why should I, as a type Five, embark on sixty days of devotions?

Whether you have just realized you are a type Five on the Enneagram or have come to terms with that reality, you've probably thought at one point or another, *Okay, but what now? I get that I'm a thinker, I struggle with low energy, I have an investigative nature, I value competency, and I have an insatiable thirst for knowledge about my topics of interest. The question is, how do I take this self-awareness and turn it into practical transformation?*

Some Enneagram teachers will tell you that you need only to focus on self-actualization and pull yourself up by your proverbial bootstraps to grow out of your worst behaviors. They say things like, "Meditate!" or "Focus on yourself!" or "Step out of your comfort zone!"

However, I'm here to offer a different foundation for growth. As Christians, we know that we are flawed, sinful, and far from God's intended plan for humanity. The hymn "Come Thou Fount of Every Blessing includes the lyrics, "Prone to wander, Lord, I feel it." This speaks to the reality of our hearts and their rebellious nature toward our Savior.

This wandering is the problem, sin is the problem, we are the problem! So, anyone who tells us that we ought to focus on ourselves to find growth will only lead us to more confusion. We may even find ourselves back where we started, as we go around and around this idea of focusing on self.

But we are not without hope. Philippians 1:6 says: "*I am sure of this, that he who began a good work in you will bring it to completion at the day of Jesus Christ.*" On the very day you acknowledged Jesus as your Savior, repented from your sin, and dedicated your life to Him, He began a good work in your life. This work is called sanctification, which is the act of becoming holy. Your sanctification will not be finished here on earth, but you are in the process of becoming, day by day, moment by moment, only by the Holy Spirit's work and power within you.

We might not know how to articulate it, but this work of sanctification is the growth and change for which we long. All of us know we are not who we want to be. Reflecting on the human condition in Romans 7:15, Paul said, "*For I do not understand my own actions. For I do not do what I want, but I do the very thing I hate.*" Isn't that the truth? I don't want to be greedy about my time, but what other option is there when I don't have the same amount of energy as everyone else seems to have?

We all know we have this haunting *potential* that always seems just a little out of reach. We all have this nagging feeling that we are created for more...but how do we get there? Only by God's grace and power within us can we rest in His sanctifying work and trust Him for the growth and potential of bringing glory to Him day by day. Only God can sanctify us, but it is our responsibility to be "*slaves of righteousness*" (Romans 6:18) and obey Him.

Over the next sixty days, we want to take you day by day through what God says about *your specific problems as a Five* and how He wants to lovingly sanctify you into being more like Jesus.

The lens of the Enneagram gives us a great starting point for your specific pain points and strengths. We will use those to encourage you in the areas that God is reflected through you and in the areas that you need to lay down your instincts and let Him change you.

Some of these topics might be hard, but we hope that you'll let the tension you feel in your heart open you up to change. This is where our obedience comes in. We all have blind spots and areas we are more comfortable leaving in the dark, but God desires so much more for us. So ask Him to help you release your grip on those areas, bring them into the light, and experience the freedom of repentance.

Maybe I'm just a heretic of my own making

I've been waging wars
That were never meant to be fought
Sense and the Senseless
Endlessly battling it
Just to find peace
Or keep a piece
Of mind

I believed for so long
That my world could only exist
With one or the other
To entertain both
Would surely cost too much

So I made an enemy out of the unknown
Unknowingly keeping myself
From knowing me [the truth]
From the one thing
That could set me free

But now I think and I feel
Thoughts about feelings
Feelings about thoughts
Foreign friends, meeting at last
Head and Heart in harmony

Free.

—*Arielle Bacon*

YOUR GUIDES FOR THIS JOURNEY

You'll be hearing from three other writers and Enneagram coaches in the days ahead. The days in which no author is listed are written by me. On other days, I have asked two Enneagram Fives and fellow Enneagram coach to help you on your path.

JARRETT BRADLEY

Jarrett Bradley is an Enneagram Five who loves to think about...stuff. Homebuilding, stocks, working out, and counseling are the topics his mind frequents, but, most importantly, he tries to think about what it looks like to serve the kingdom of God through the skills God has given him and then do it. He has a degree in Christian counseling and currently works as a carpenter. He lives in Pennsylvania, where he enjoys spending time with his wife, Alison Bradley, and their two children.

ALISON BRADLEY

Alison is an Enneagram Nine who has always loved stories, whether it is reading them or helping others listen to their own. You'll often find her outside, making a bouquet of flowers, or inside, relaxing at the local library. She also loves being around her kitchen table in Bucks County, Pennsylvania, with her husband, Jarrett Bradley, and two kids, often eating gluten-free, chocolate chip pancakes.

ANNA YATES

Anna is an Enneagram Five wing Four, tea enthusiast, book devourer, nature-walk taker, listener, thinker, growing empathizer, and Enneagram coach and writer. With a background in social media marketing, Anna loves to explore the Enneagram, listen to others' stories, and fuse the two with spiritual and scriptural insights and practices. She's passionate about helping others connect with God in a deeper way and follow Him. In her free time, she loves enjoying sunny Florida outdoors, scouting out the best gluten-free goodies, and spending quality time with loved ones and her kitten, Rosalita.

10 DAYS OF KNOWLEDGE
How You Uniquely Reflect God's Wisdom

• • • • • • • • • • **DAY 1**

Driven to "Know"

> *For the protection of wisdom is like the protection of money,*
> *and the advantage of knowledge is that wisdom preserves*
> *the life of him who has it.*
> (Ecclesiastes 7:12)

As a Five, you are motivated by competency and the search to understand the unknown. You will have a question, search out answers, analyze what you find, and either come to a conclusion or keep your mind open to more input. Whatever your analysis leads you to, this cycle will be no stranger to you as you receive information, have questions, and seek out answers.

It may seem odd to you, but most of the population doesn't want to gain information they won't use. They find *Jeopardy* facts pointless to know; if they are never going to actually fly an airplane, they aren't interested in knowing how it works; and they quickly dismiss any knowledge that doesn't have a designated purpose or practicality in their everyday life.

This is where your brain varies drastically from that of most people. There is a certain adrenaline that comes with the pursuit of knowledge, and that's what makes it feel fun to you. As a Four, I've said this many times of my own Five wing, but for Fives, there is no kind of information that is bad information. It's all just information, and you'll either use it or not—but you're never sorry to have gained the information in the first place.

This search for knowledge is an unending one, as questions, more knowledge, and more research will always be there. This is a big part of who you are and is a strength that is needed in our society, families, and churches.

Your brain is a gift, your motivation is a gift, and your presence is a gift.

SHIFT IN FOCUS

What are three topics that you've researched in depth?

1. _____

2. _____

3. _____

What are three opinions you've reconsidered?

1. _____

2. _____

3. _____

How have these six things preserved or helped you in some unforeseen way?

DAY 2 • • • • • • • • • • •

Knowledge's Relationship to Wisdom
By Jarrett Bradley

The fear of the LORD is the beginning of wisdom,
and the knowledge of the Holy One is insight.
(Proverbs 9:10)

Proverbs repeatedly tells us that *"the fear of the LORD is the beginning of wisdom,"* but what does it mean to *"fear the LORD"*? Certainly, there is a literal fear. Any individual in the Bible who had an experience of God was usually stricken with tremendous fear. However, fright alone does not constitute wisdom, for if it did, grizzly bears and sharks might be our new mentors. Beyond fright, there is another layer to the fear of the Lord.

Part of knowing God is recognizing His omnipotence: His unlimited, infinite power. Consider for a moment that the very atoms that constitute the hands you use to hold this book could, in an instant, be willed out of existence by God. Consider that, should God so choose, the laws of gravity could be instantaneously suspended, and we would find ourselves floating endlessly into space. Political upheavals, famine, pestilence—the things we fear as a society—cannot hold a candle to the power wielded by the infinite possibilities of the Lord.

Truly internalizing God's omnipotence and power can bring us to the real beginning of wisdom: humility. Our genuine lack of real power and control, our utter helplessness in light of God's power, will make us humble. Wisdom, ultimately, is a form of humility induced by recognizing the truth of who God is. Even more humbling is the gospel reality that this incredible, all-powerful God has called us His friends, His children, and His heirs through Jesus's life, death, and resurrection. The gospel, just as much as God's power, can wring out the pride within us and replace it with humility—if we let it.

Wisdom that comes from the humility of understanding who God is gives meaningful direction to knowledge. But what does that mean? To start, it is important to recognize that the temptation with knowledge alone is to use it pridefully—to take information and use it for our own means, or, perhaps more disastrously, to find our meaning and purpose within knowledge. If my self-worth comes from the knowledge I have, then, functionally, that knowledge is my god. And if knowledge is my god, then misuse and abuse of that knowledge is sure to follow.

However, to have the kind of humble wisdom that comes from understanding God's tremendous power, followed by His tremendous love, gives meaningful direction to how we use knowledge. If the gospel is the truth, why seek affirmation from others through the things we know? Why pursue personal gain with our knowledge when the all-powerful God who created those things has called us His children? What greater joy is there than to ask God how best to use the knowledge we do have to further His kingdom in wisdom, and to delight in what follows?

Bear in mind that knowledge alone does not necessitate wisdom, nor vice versa. However, it is better to be a dullard who has wisdom than to be a fool with knowledge, and both are certainly possible. A skiff with a destination is better than a yacht lost at sea. But imagine—*imagine!*—the marvelous things that could be done with knowledge drenched in wisdom. Oh, that we would become those kinds of people.

SHIFT IN FOCUS

What would it look like to work with God using the knowledge you already have?

Does the idea of working with God sound like it would interfere with the plans you have, or does the idea of working with God excite you?

• • • • • • • • • • • DAY 3

How You Reflect God

Then God said, "Let us make man in our image, after our likeness."
(Genesis 1:26)

Dear Five, do you know you uniquely reflect God? In Genesis, God says that He made us in His image. Now, this doesn't mean our bodies look like His, but rather that we reflect His image by reflecting parts of God's character. It's not a perfect reflection; in fact, it's rippled and marred. However, a familiarity, a family resemblance, is still plainly evident between God and His creation.

God is so mighty, majestic, and perfect that none of us can reflect every part of Him, so we see His attributes scattered throughout the entire population. Each of us is reflecting Him in unique and very important ways. This is why we hear about each of us being a part of God's body in 1 Corinthians 12:27, Romans 12:5, and Ephesians 5:30. Each of us is uniquely made for a divine purpose; each of us alone is just a piece, but together we are whole.

As a Five, you reflect our Father's love of knowledge, His wisdom, His unbiased nature, His faithfulness, His desire for truth, and His self-control, just to name a few. These are attributes of God that your soul recognizes, runs toward, and acts in, especially when you're healthy.

When you act out of your desire for knowledge, have self-control, or choose objectivity over your own emotional biases, you're showing the world a part of God that brings glory to Him. Showing the world the very nature of God is the greatest honor we inherit as part of His creation, and as Christians, this is our very purpose.

I find that it's easy to focus on the ways we don't reflect God, and our sin is often so loud and shameful, it demands center stage in the thoughts we have about ourselves.

However, have you ever thought about how dwelling on how you reflect God brings glory to Him?

Like a father who brags about his child's musical talent that mirrors his own, God, like a good father, is proud and delighted in the ways we are similar. Thinking about these things, and thanking Him for them, are important for having the right attitude toward ourselves as humans. We are humble, small, fickle, and sinful...yet adopted, created, and loved beyond measure.

SHIFT IN FOCUS

Spend a couple of moments reflecting on and thanking God for the ways you reflect Him. If these words reflect your heart, please borrow them:

Dear heavenly Father, thank You for making me like You. Help me to notice more and more every day the gifts that You have given me and how I can glorify You with them. I want others to look at me and see a glimmer of You. Thank You for helping me do that. Amen.

My favorite reflection of God I can see in myself is:

• • • • • • • • • • • **DAY 4**

God Delights in Knowledge

Have you not known? Have you not heard? The LORD is the everlasting God, the Creator of the ends of the earth. He does not faint or grow weary; his understanding is unsearchable.
(Isaiah 40:28)

God's understanding, His knowledge, and His wisdom is unsearchable. It's overwhelming to even think about this. He is the One who created knowledge, our brains, and the ability for us to learn. This is something I have found that Fives understand well, and I think it is why Fives tend to naturally view themselves humbly.

When you are drawn to a pursuit of knowledge, you can't help but be in awe of the Creator of knowledge and the Creator of whatever you happen to be studying again and again.

First Corinthians 14:33 reads: *"For God is not a God of confusion."* We see the truth of this even in His creation. God's creation makes sense, and we are continually putting together the pieces of this vast puzzle. Mathematics, astronomy, engineering, economics, psychology—there is a myriad of areas of study where we are still figuring out how God's creation works, and it fascinates us.

What we see throughout Scripture is a God who is not an absent Creator. He did not create and forget, He is not distant, and I can't help but think that, like a parent who delights in their small child learning, God delights in us learning as well.

Second Timothy 2:7 reads: *"Think over what I say, for the Lord will give you understanding in everything."* Not only does God care enough to create an environment that is mentally stimulating, calls to the glory of a Creator, and provides us with delight, but He is also the One who gives us understanding.

We can see this throughout history as we are faced with problem after problem, and understanding seems to come out of nowhere. We discover, win battles, and learn all to the glory of a God who not only delights in knowledge, but is the Creator of knowledge.

SHIFT IN FOCUS

Can you think of a time when knowledge seemed to be given to you when you needed it most?

What part does humility play in your pursuit of knowledge?

Do you often feel in awe and humbled in your pursuit of knowledge, or do you feel puffed up and powerful?

• • • • • • • • • • **DAY 5**

God's Gift of Wisdom
By Alison Bradley

If any of you lacks wisdom, let him ask God, who gives generously
to all without reproach, and it will be given him.
(James 1:5)

There are many things we ask God for, but I love noticing that one of the things we are told the Lord gives generously and without hesitation is wisdom. In this same chapter in James, we read about God the Father's heart that loves to give gifts: *"Every good gift and every perfect gift is from above, coming down from the Father of lights"* (James 1:17).

In this season of parenting, I have lots of needs coming from my two small children. Although I don't welcome whining or complaints, I truly celebrate when my children ask for my knowledge to help them. I love it when they welcome my help to work through something that is new to them or that they've never encountered before. I can't help but imagine the parent heart of God responding in a similar way when we humbly come to Him asking for help and wisdom in something new to us or beyond our abilities.

Dear Five, this generous gift of wisdom that God offers us is reflected in you. I'm so grateful for the enthusiasm and gentleness with which I've been taught by the Fives in my life. When you're reflecting God with your wisdom, you're not shaming someone for not knowing something. You're delighted to find that they're a willing learner. You're happy to share your knowledge. You want to help them live well. You're glad for them to discover a better way of doing things.

SHIFT IN FOCUS

In the Old Testament, King David speaks often about how he experiences the Lord sharing wisdom and guidance with him. We see evidence throughout the Psalms of this aspect of the Lord's character. The Lord generously shares His wisdom with us, out of love, so that we might live the best kind of life.

+ *"You make known to me the path of life."* (Psalm 16:11)

+ *"The law of the* LORD *is perfect, reviving the soul; the testimony of the* LORD *is sure, making wise the simple."* (Psalm 19:7)

+ *"Good and upright is the* LORD; *therefore he instructs sinners in the way. He leads the humble in what is right, and teaches the humble his way."* (Psalm 25:8–9)

+ *"For you are my rock and my fortress; and for your name's sake you lead and guide me."* (Psalm 31:3)

Which verse do you find yourself most drawn to? If you are able, I encourage you to go read the whole psalm to see the verse in its context.

Pause to respond to the Lord's generous gift of wisdom. What would you like to tell the Lord about the wisdom that He gives? What would you like to tell Him about being given the ability to reflect this part of His character to others?

• • • • • • • • • • • DAY 6

Solomon and Wisdom Stewarded

*And God gave Solomon wisdom and understanding beyond measure,
and breadth of mind like the sand on the seashore, so that Solomon's
wisdom surpassed the wisdom of all the people of the east and all
the wisdom of Egypt. For he was wiser than all other men, wiser
than Ethan the Ezrahite, and Heman, Calcol, and Darda, the sons
of Mahol, and his fame was in all the surrounding nations. He also
spoke 3,000 proverbs, and his songs were 1,005. He spoke of trees,
from the cedar that is in Lebanon to the hyssop that grows out of the
wall. He spoke also of beasts, and of birds, and of reptiles, and of fish.*
(1 Kings 4:29–34)

The biblical story of King Solomon is one I go back to over and
over. Solomon was the son of King David and heir to the throne
of Israel. He was handsome, smart, and, being a prince, he probably never wanted for much.

When his father died, Solomon became king, and God
appeared to Solomon and asked him what he wanted. Solomon
asked for wisdom. God was so pleased with Solomon's response
that He vowed to increase Solomon's wealth and fame as well.

Solomon had the honor of building a temple for God in
Israel. This was an honor David sought, but God told him no
because David was a man of war and thus his hands were soaked
with blood. So God told David that his son Solomon would be
the one to build the Lord's house.

Solomon reigned during a time of great wealth and power in Israel. He was esteemed far and wide, known for his wisdom not only in matters of dispute but also in writings, art, and zoology.

Before you start envying Solomon or wishing God would bestow you with a supernatural wisdom gift, remember that there is a plot twist in Solomon's story. The Bible gives this heartbreaking heading for 1 Kings 11: *"Solomon turns from the LORD."*

My heart always cries "What? No! Why?" when I read this. Solomon had everything; God had blessed him beyond measure. Solomon spoke to God in a way you and I probably never will. So what happened? Gluttony happened. Solomon had everything, but he still wanted more, and that desire would ultimately lead his heart astray.

You see, Solomon had a problem with greed and gluttony. Not just gluttony around wealth, chariots, horses, wisdom, fame, and drink, although the Bible talks about all those things, but mainly around women. Solomon is recorded as having seven hundred wives and three hundred concubines. This man had more wives than almost any man in recorded history, and they turned his heart away from God.

History will show you time and time again that those of us who have everything never feel like we have enough. This isn't just a problem for you, but it's a problem for whoever you idolize or wish you could be as well. Enough is never enough, and this goes for knowledge too. When you long for competence, you may become distracted by those who know more than you do and make you feel less than. But more is never truly the answer to our heart's cry.

No amount of knowledge, esteem, or *more* of any kind will ever fill the God-shaped hole in your heart.

SHIFT IN FOCUS

Do you fall victim to the lie that if you had more, you would finally feel fully competent?

What is that *more* in your life?

Name three things you think would allow you to feel competent:

1. _____
2. _____
3. _____

DAY 7 • • • • • • • • • •

Living as a Lifelong Student
By Jarrett Bradley

Whoever corrects a scoffer gets himself abuse, and he who reproves
a wicked man incurs injury. Do not reprove a scoffer, or he will hate
you; reprove a wise man, and he will love you. Give instruction to a
wise man, and he will be still wiser; teach a righteous man, and he
will increase in learning.
(Proverbs 9:7–9)

What does it look like to be someone who is perpetually teach-able? Proverbs 9 speaks to us about both sides of the coin: one person who has become unteachable, and another who continues to learn. It is easy to look at the proverb and see the stupidity of becoming the "scoffer" and the wisdom in becoming the "wise man." However, we have the advantage of reading the text from afar. It is quite another thing to allow the words to enter our heart and judge us for who we are *and* who we are becoming. Will we choose the path of the scoffer, or will we choose the path of the wise person?

Our first question should naturally be, "Why in the heck would anyone *want* to become a scoffer when it's so obviously the wrong choice?" The answer—perhaps just as naturally—is that no one in the history of the planet has ever aspired to become a scoffer...and yet it has happened, and it can most certainly happen to us. Perhaps our real questions should be, "What is in the heart of our proverbial scoffer? And what drives the *wicked man* to reject correction?"

The misalignment in the heart of the scoffer is undoubtedly that the desire to be right has usurped the desire for truth. It has become more important to protect the ego than to learn what may need changing in the heart. This state creates a porcupine-like character: quills out, ready to retaliate, or—more likely—to come off as so abrasive that none dare approach (even in love) for fear of getting stabbed by mere proximity.

Fundamentally, this state of the heart is about pride and, for the Enneagram Five, it is usually pride in the form of competency, or being perceived as competent. It can be embarrassing to feel incompetent, but that embarrassment only extends as deep as we have placed our meaning and purpose in what we believe we know. When our own knowledge is where we find our meaning, we are sure to become prickly whenever something, or someone, threatens it. It is only through Christ that our inner scoffer can be axed.

Through the gospel, Jesus offers us freedom from the need to be seen as competent. We are already loved by God, and to internalize that truth gives us leave to become a wise person—the kind of person who can embrace insightful rebuke and become ever wiser. In the gospel, our identity no longer needs to be wrapped up in being right or being seen as intelligent. We could be as dumb as a stump and still be loved by the King.

SHIFT IN FOCUS

Can you think of a recent time when you were agitated by someone correcting you?

Regardless of whether the person was right or wrong—since the feeling of agitation is what concerns us—where do you think that feeling came from? What was stirred in your heart?

• • • • • • • • • • DAY 8

Right Brain vs. Left Brain

For we are his workmanship, created in Christ Jesus for good works,
which God prepared beforehand, that we should walk in them.
(Ephesians 2:10)

The difference between your left brain and right brain is a concept with which most people are at least vaguely familiar. But if you need a refresher, it goes like this: if you are left-brain dominant, you are more analytical, logical, and methodical in your thinking. The left brain is the side we use when we are proofreading or trying to learn a new math concept. On the other hand, if you are right-brain dominant, you're more emotional and creative. You use your right brain when you're painting or imagining a scene in a story you're reading.

You probably knew coming into this day that you are left-brain dominant, but did you know that you have a really cool access point to the right brain as well?

Enneagram Fours and Fives can cross what some call the *abyss* or *brain divide* between left brain and right brain. Fives are representative of the left brain on the Enneagram, and Fours are representative of the right brain. However, these two types, though vastly different, share the ability to have a wing of the other. This wing is crossing the wide gap at the bottom of the Enneagram diagram, which is symbolic for the gap between thinking and feeling, realism and imagination, facts and creativity, nonfiction and fiction, left brain and right brain.

Even if you are dominant in your Six wing, you still have access to your Four wing. This balances what would otherwise be an excess in left-brain thinking. You need your right brain, and right-brain activities probably help you relax if you have a left-brain job. For example, perhaps you read works of fiction after working all day as an accountant, or you do something creative with your hands after working all day as an editor.

Left-brain thinking brings order to the world and is the thinking by which everything can make sense. Your left-brain dominance is an important and much-needed way of thinking in a world that doesn't seem to make much sense.

This being true, it's also important to acknowledge your need and leaning toward the right brain in order to appreciate the giftings of what the right brain brings to the world. One way of thinking isn't better than the other. They're just different, and God made every personality with its specific flaws and strengths for a purpose.

SHIFT IN FOCUS

Who in your life is right-brain dominant?

What specific things are they really good at? What do you admire about them?

Do you think you have a dominant Four wing?

In what ways do you see a leaning toward the right brain in your life?

• • • • • • • • • • • DAY 9

Finding Truth in Reconsideration

But test everything; hold fast what is good.
(1 Thessalonians 5:21)

To reconsider (or consider again) means to take an idea or thought process you've held for a while and bring it back into the interrogation chair. You may have held some ideas and choices for so long that you don't even know where they came from. This is why reconsideration is a great spiritual practice to have in your arsenal.

This topic is one I've learned the most about from Enneagram Five Knox McCoy, author of the book *All Things Reconsidered*. Through his thoughtful and gentle prompting, I've learned to think of reconsideration not as something that I need to be given permission to do, but something I *get to do* with the Holy Spirit as an adult.

We can reconsider topics ranging from silly and lighthearted—e.g., *Is Joe the best singer among the Jonas Brothers? Is three cups of coffee a day a reasonable amount?*—to much heavier topics, such as, *Is this friendship one that I really want to have in my life? What do I really believe about human nature?* What might've prompted a quick yes last year might make you pause today. Reconsideration might come upon you with a life change when someone challenges a belief you've never reconsidered, or just by happenstance.

I firmly know and trust that, no matter how, when, what, or why you are reconsidering, God can handle your questions.

Faith doesn't mean holding out your hands for any belief your pastor subscribes to, eyes closed, with a smile on your face. You are allowed to have questions, search for answers on your own, and invite the Holy Spirit to be a part of that process with you.

SHIFT IN FOCUS

Pick two topics, one silly and one serious, that you want to reconsider over the next three months:

1. _____

2. _____

The beautiful thing about having a living, breathing relationship with God is that we can trust Him with our big questions. With Him, we can test what we have always believed, and with Him, we can find new understanding or become firmer in what we've always known but never fully understood.

• • • • • • • • • • • **DAY 10**

Finding Truth Guided by the Holy Spirit
By Jarrett Bradley

For my thoughts are not your thoughts, neither are your ways my
ways, declares the LORD.
(Isaiah 55:8)

And they were all filled with the Holy Spirit and began to speak in
other tongues as the Spirit gave them utterance.
(Acts 2:4)

When Jesus brought His message to the world, people were floored. No one, from the highest authority to the lowliest peasant, had a clue what to make of the Man and the message He proclaimed. One of the most striking things about the message Jesus brought was that the individuals who were expected to have the best and most cutting-edge knowledge of God were not merely at a loss for what to do with the person and message of Jesus, but they actively worked to kill Him—and, eventually, they did.

Consider, for a moment, how incredibly intelligent and amazingly well-read the Pharisees were. These individuals could quote the first five books of the Bible verbatim (think about that!) and were constantly mulling over the meaning of the Scriptures. The church today seems to have largely written off the Pharisees as the classic example of stupidity and arrogance: idiots who missed the big picture when it was literally standing right in front of them. Most of the Pharisees may have missed the message, but they were anything but idiots. Fools, perhaps, but not idiots.

We should not assume that just because we have a historical perspective we are incapable of committing the same mistakes the Pharisees committed. God's ways are not our ways, and His thoughts are not our thoughts. But if that is the case, and even smart folks like the Pharisees could miss the big picture, what hope do we have of discerning God's kingdom reality for what it really is?

Enter the Holy Spirit. To follow Jesus is to have real and immediate access to the Holy Spirit. Knowledge alone can only take us so far in the pursuit of God and His kingdom; eventually, the way we perceive and interpret reality goes askew to one degree or another. The Holy Spirit is there to offer correction so long as we are willing to humble ourselves and ask for it.

It is worth noting, as well, that the kind of truth the Holy Spirit directs us in can be anything, but it is generally in the realm of questions concerning goodness. What is the good life? Who is really well off? How do I love the person in front of me at this very moment? Truth, in such contexts, is not usually as cut and dry as we would like it to be. However, the answers we arrive at through the Holy Spirit can produce a wondrous life...though not always the one we may have imagined we would want. The kingdom of God tends to turn our expectations on their head, but the result, if we allow it, is both a marvel and a beauty to behold.

SHIFT IN FOCUS

How would you describe your relationship with the Holy Spirit?

Do you think about the person of the Holy Spirit as someone who you have access to and someone you can speak to even now?

Take some time to speak to the Spirit about what you've been thinking about, even if it seems mundane.

10 DAYS OF GREED
How the Enemy Wants You to Stop Reflecting God

DAY 11 • • • • • • • • • •

What Is a Deadly Sin?

If anyone is caught in any transgression, you who are spiritual should restore him in a spirit of gentleness. Keep watch on yourself, lest you too be tempted.
(Galatians 6:1)

Although the wording or specific idea for the "seven deadly sins" is not in the Bible, the list of them has been used by Christians for ages. The classification of seven deadly sins that we know today was first penned by a monk named Evagrius Ponticus who lived from AD 345–399.

This list has gone through many changes since its origination, but it has remained a helpful way for us to name the common vices that keep us in chains.

When these seven sins are paired with specific Enneagram numbers (plus two extra sins to make nine), they give us a better idea of the specific vices that may be tripping us up again and again. This is important because these problems are often blind spots in our lives. Their exposure leads us to repentance, better health, and greater unity with Christ, which is the greatest thing learning about our Enneagram number can do for us.

Here are the deadly sins early Enneagram teachers paired with each type:

1. Anger
2. Pride
3. Deceit
4. Envy
5. Greed
6. Fear
7. Gluttony
8. Lust
9. Sloth

Struggling with one of these sins dominantly does not mean that you do not struggle with all of them. If we are honest with ourselves and humble, we can all recognize ourselves in each of the sins listed. However, your dominant deadly sin is a specific tool Satan will use to distract the world from seeing how you reflect God.

For Fives, the deadly sin you struggle with most is greed. Whether or not you recognize greed in your own life as you're thinking about it now, I entreat you to give great thought to it in these next ten days.

Exposing blind spots in our life can feel a lot like ripping off a bandage that we might prefer to leave on, but what's underneath is God-honoring and beautiful.

SHIFT IN FOCUS

Spend some time contemplating and praying about what greed might look like in your life.

Does it surprise you to see that specific sin printed next to your Enneagram number?

• • • • • • • • • • • DAY 12

What Is Greed?

You will be enriched in every way to be generous in every way.
(2 Corinthians 9:11)

Greed is a desire or strong longing for more. It is often a desire for more money, but when we speak of greed in an Enneagram context, we mean much more than that.

Greed or avarice, which is extreme greed, is the deadly sin of Fives. This refers not just to hoarding money but to the tight hold that Fives are tempted to have on their time, money, food, emotions, talents, or really anything else that could be a good gift when freely given. Greed is the action of believing that God will not replenish you and that you need to take care of yourself.

When Scripture tells us in 2 Corinthians 9:11, *"You will be enriched in every way to be generous in every way,"* it isn't saying you'll get something in return; rather, it is acknowledging who our time, money, emotions, and so on *really* belong to. When you live believing that everything is a gift from God, you won't feel the need to hoard because you know who replenishes your stores.

Greed distracts people from recognizing God's reflection in Fives because it makes Fives inaccessible to others. The enemy wants Fives to hoard their talents, time, and emotions so that they are the only ones who enjoy the imaging of God they reflect. Fives are such a gift to the rest of us when they trust God to replenish them and are able to give without fear.

Greed cuts in line, greed doesn't give when it should, and greed always wants more. Enough is never enough where greed is concerned. It's an insatiable master. Jesus tells us, *"No one can serve two masters, for either he will hate the one and love the other, or he will be devoted to the one and despise the other. You cannot serve God and money"* (Matthew 6:24). You cannot love God fully and hoard everything He has given you for yourself. If you do, you're choosing greed over God.

SHIFT IN FOCUS

Pray and ask God to search your heart and expose any part of you that is trying to serve both greed and Him. If these words reflect your heart, please borrow them:

Dear heavenly Father, I bring my heart, actions, and thoughts to You now. Please search me and know me. Expose any areas where greed has taken root, and bring me to humble repentance. Help me to grow in this area and continue to expose greed that I wasn't aware of so I can look more like You. Amen.

• • • • • • • • • • • DAY 13

"But I'm Not Greedy!"

One gives freely, yet grows all the richer; another withholds
what he should give, and only suffers want.
(Proverbs 11:24)

We typically have a picture of greed that comes from mob bosses, Old Testament kings, and corporate guys in suits who will backstab, lie, cheat, and steal in order to get ahead. But that's not always what greed looks like. Greed doesn't necessarily come out of a wicked and gross part of our hearts. Not everyone who experiences greed is going out of their way to gain in order to feel rich and important.

Sometimes, greed is a reaction to a wound, a strong desire or compulsion toward accumulation, especially of money or something you once lacked.

We've seen this in people who lived through the Great Depression (1929–1939). They saw normal life slip away and the food, clothing, and extras they once enjoyed became limited and expensive. For many, this caused a scarcity mindset. If something they once longed for became available or was a bargain, even if they didn't need it or already had plenty, they would buy it and store it—because it might not always be there. The scars of once being deprived are deep and cause this kind of greed to take root.

We now have multiple shows on TV about hoarders who compulsively collect and store all types of things. The one factor these people all have in common is pain and trying to fill a void—either an emotional void or a practical void—by filling it in excess.

Greed can be purposeful, destructive, and self-focused, but I have a feeling this is not what greed looks like for you. Maybe your greed is coming out of a place of pain and lack. If this is true for you, I am sorry that you know such pain. Looking to God's Word, we see assurance that He will supply our every need. Turn to Him and let Him fill any void in your heart.

SHIFT IN FOCUS

What have you lacked?

How does that season or moment of lacking play a role in how you protect yourself from ever lacking?

• • • • • • • • • • • • **DAY 14**

What the Bible Says about Greed

But those who desire to be rich fall into temptation, into a snare, into many senseless and harmful desires that plunge people into ruin and destruction.
(1 Timothy 6:9)

Dear Five, where do you desire to be rich? We all desire to be rich in one way or another, and usually this desire is around our need for comfort.

If I had more free time, I wouldn't be this tired or stressed. I want to be rich in freedom.

If I had a close relationship, I wouldn't feel rejected and lonely. I want to be rich in love.

If I had more money, I wouldn't need to worry about my finances. I want to be rich with money.

If I had more energy, maybe people would like me more. I want to be rich in energy.

We want our lives to be easier and we don't want to feel like we are swimming against the current. Usually we have an idea of what one thing we need in order to achieve the comfort we seek. (If we don't, commercials will try to tell us what that one thing is. Spoiler alert: it's a new car.)

There are many things that can cause longing within us and the ache of greed that accompanies it.

Greed tickles our ear, strokes our pride, and lays a snare for our soul with a few sweet words: *I know what you need. If only you had this, then you would have enough. Just a little more. Why is it so easy for them? Everything you need is just a little out of reach.*

The Bible has some stern words about greed, particularly the love of money.

> *For the love of money is a root of all kinds of evils. It is through this craving that some have wandered away from the faith and pierced themselves with many pangs.*
>
> (1 Timothy 6:10)

> *Keep your life free from love of money, and be content with what you have, for he has said, "I will never leave you nor forsake you."*   (Hebrews 13:5)

Why would reminding us that God *"will never leave us or forsake us"* be an antidote for greed? Because greed assumes we are not taken care of, greed assumes we need more, and greed assumes God is not a good and loving Father.

SHIFT IN FOCUS

Where in your life are you assuming that you won't be taken care of?

Memorize Matthew 7:9–11 or write it out and display it somewhere where you will see it every day:

> *Which one of you, if his son asks him for bread, will give him a stone? Or if he asks for a fish, will give him a serpent?*

If you then, who are evil, know how to give good gifts to your children, how much more will your Father who is in heaven give good things to those who ask him!

DAY 15 • • • • • • • • • • •

Greed and the Story of Jonah
By Anna Yates

But it displeased Jonah exceedingly, and he was angry. And he prayed to the LORD and said, "O LORD, is not this what I said when I was yet in my country? That is why I made haste to flee to Tarshish; for I knew that you are a gracious God and merciful, slow to anger and abounding in steadfast love, and relenting from disaster. Therefore now, O LORD, please take my life from me, for it is better for me to die than to live."
(Jonah 4:1–3)

Dear Five, there is enough love and life for you, too. God is taking care of you.

I relate to Jonah. Even though I'm not called to preach repentance to a city of Assyrians, I too can become greedy with the gifts given to me.

Greediness comes in many forms. For Jonah, it looked like hoarding the plant God gave him in the wilderness and hoarding the good news of God's gracious and forgiving nature. For me, it looks like hoarding energy, time with loved ones, time alone, knowledge, and so on. Greediness at its core is a scarcity mindset. It focuses only on what I don't have and the fear that there won't be enough. It makes me hold tightly to what I have so I don't lose it.

So why didn't Jonah want the Ninevites to experience God's forgiveness? Later in Israel's history, the Assyrians invaded, overtook the Israelites, and carried them into slavery. But during Jonah's time, they were still a rising power. I think a scarcity mindset kept Jonah from generosity. Maybe he had a hard time accepting the fullness of God's grace for himself, and so he had a hard time sharing.

Again, I relate to Jonah. So often I fear that there's not enough strength, not enough forgiveness, not enough love for me, too. I fear there's a limited amount of resources, and some for others means less for me. I fear that my weaknesses—the places I'm not capable enough—prevent me from receiving the good things God has for me. I fear that my lack makes me unloved and unusable.

In reality, just the opposite is true: if I were perfectly sufficient in myself, I wouldn't need an overwhelming grace. When I bring my weakness, messiness, fears, and lack to God, I open up space to receive the presence that covers everything. God brings me into alignment with His heart and purpose and uses my surrender for His kingdom. I can learn from Jonah by holding the things I've been given with an open hand.

God doesn't give up on a heart that has turned toward Him. And His presence is always enough for me.

SHIFT IN FOCUS

Read Jonah 3:10–4:11.

In what areas do you feel yourself having difficulty with generosity right now?

What fears lie beneath those feelings?

How are you seeing grace show up?

How can you abide in God's presence today to experience His sufficiency?

If these words reflect your heart, please borrow them:

Dear heavenly Father, I recognize my need for Your grace today. I want to let go of the things I'm holding onto too tightly so I can experience Your sufficiency. In this moment, I let Your presence trickle into my heart and mind, filling the parched cracks and smoothing over the broken places. In humble silence, I accept Your forgiveness for my mistakes, Your strength for my failures, Your love for my entire being. I accept Your delight in me. Give me the generosity to share the same grace to others today. Amen.

• • • • • • • • • • • **DAY 16**

Greed and Energy
By Anna Yates

*Nevertheless, I am continually with you; you hold my right hand.
You guide me with your counsel, and afterward you will receive me
to glory. Whom have I in heaven but you? And there is nothing on
earth that I desire besides you. My flesh and my heart may fail, but
God is the strength of my heart and my portion forever.*
(Psalm 73:23–26)

Let me just say: I love kids. But they're also extremely draining.
With three older brothers, I've partially grown up with my nieces
and nephews around. And since I still live at home, I see *plenty*
of my seven- and eight-year-old nephews during sleepovers and
Saturday hangouts.

When my nephews wake me up at 9 a.m. on a Saturday
morning literally screaming, or show up like a tornado at my
house after a long workday, I'm less than excited. Britton and
Grant learned fast that screaming is a surefire way to bring out
Aunt Anna's grump.

So I talked with my parents about how it drains me to even
be around my nephews—a big step for a Self-Preservation Five.

My parents (an Enneagram Two and a Six) didn't understand, but they agreed to ask me if the nephews could come over
for a visit. For years, the conversations kept happening. My parents often remembered to ask me, but it turned out to be more
of a formality. Then I'd get upset and withdraw. I felt like my

parents were choosing their grandkids over me, and they felt like I was rejecting them and my nephews. Finally, the tension came to a head in one conflict, and I had to face how deeply my anger and withdrawal hurt my parents. I also realized how deeply I was hurt by what felt like their disrespect of my rights and rejection of my needs.

Afterward, as I prayed with worship music, I heard God speaking. It was, frankly, a little shattering. He told me, "Anna, this isn't something you get to fight about anymore. I understand how you feel. I see your rights and needs. But you can't rob your parents of their ministry or your nephews of the joy of being close to their grandparents. I'm calling you to let go of your rights."

It was a gentle and affirming message. During a solid hour of crying and praying, I surrendered that right, that need for a quiet space, for energy, even for respect. It was painful. Like Eustace in C. S. Lewis's *The Voyage of the Dawn Treader*, I was being stripped of pride and greed.

I still sometimes feel strained when my nephews are around, but I now have peace in nonattachment. I can withdraw healthily when I'm exhausted or stressed and can give more energy. I can cling less to my needs and more to the Source who fills me up because He's enough for me.

SHIFT IN FOCUS

Read Psalms 73.

If these words reflect your heart, please borrow them:

Dear heavenly Father, thank You for seeing me and understanding me in my weakness and exhaustion. Thank You for making me the way I am and giving me the bravery to speak up for my needs. Give me the bravery and humility to also release my needs and rights. I feel so lacking. I need You to fill me up. Whatever that looks like, whatever that calls for, I'm ready to let You in. I let go. Right now, fill me with Your presence and peace. Amen.

DAY 17 • • • • • • • • • • •

Greed and Stockpiling

When I am afraid, I put my trust in you. In God,
whose word I praise, in God I trust; I shall not be afraid.
What can flesh do to me?
(Psalm 56:3–4)

I've watched more Fives and Sixes than I can count on shows like *Extreme Couponing* or *Doomsday Preppers*. Although any type would have the potential to tap into the extremes found on these shows, Fives with a Six wing and Sixes with a Five wing tend to take the cake for number of appearances.

Do you have anything that you stockpile…just in case? Do you have a cellar of canned foods, a garage full of more toilet paper than you could ever use, or a full bank account, yet you still spend so much time couponing every week that it's like a part-time job?

Being a Five and feeling lacking can lead to greed. On top of that, if you have a Six wing, you long for security, which can cause you to over-prepare for worst-case scenarios. When these two types collide in a 5w6 or 6w5, we can see hoarding, extreme preparation, conspiracy theory rationalization, and stockpiling at its finest. These are some of the unhealthier traits of these types. An average 5w6 or 6w5 won't be television-show worthy. But if you are a 5w6, you might recognize this temptation in yourself.

Although preparing and taking steps to protect yourself and your loved ones can be a good and wise thing, often our preparation is a response to fear, a symptom of us trying to control what we ultimately cannot control.

The connection between fear and control is a strong one, but only in loosening our grip on what we want to control do we have the ability to take God's hand in faith.

> *Now faith is the assurance of things hoped for, the conviction of things not seen.* (Hebrews 11:1)

We don't need to be reckless and unprepared or stop having extras on hand, just in case. But if you have a tendency toward this behavior, I don't think recklessness is the extreme you'll swing toward. Instead of trying not to stockpile, go through what you have once a month and commit to gifting or donating a portion. Start small, and see what God does with your heart.

SHIFT IN FOCUS

Do you think you lean more dominant in 5w4 or 5w6?

Do you identify with having a temptation to hoard or stockpile in preparations?

Spend some time thinking through how wise preparation *and* generosity can look for you.

Where in your life are you trying to control something out of fear?

DAY 18 • • • • • • • • • • •

Greed and Knowledge

For where your treasure is, there your heart will be also.
(Matthew 6:21)

Dear Five, you are very knowledgeable. I know there is a suspicion in the back of your head that you are not, but I want you to hear this: *you are a storehouse of intelligence and insight.* I don't even know you, and I have full confidence in saying those words.

You may not know more than that one person you follow on social media or be as wise as that teacher you admire, but that does not mean you don't have something important to add to the world. With great knowledge comes great responsibility. I know it may not feel like that when you're gathering your information. Usually, the accumulation of knowledge is done for fun or for a specific purpose; but have you ever thought about being generous with what you know?

Most Fives have a humble view of their own knowledge, but the Fives who seem to know they are knowledgeable also have an air of pride. They only use their knowledge when they are being paid, or when they're correcting someone else. Nothing makes an unhealthy Five feel more competent than the feeling of superiority that comes with correcting or shaming someone else. Pride and greed are an ugly mixture in unhealthy Fives, and I do not advise operating out of both simultaneously for fear you may be on the receiving end of a well-earned punch to the nose...but I digress.

To have a right view of your own knowledge means to see it as a gift and be generous with sharing what you know. Have you ever thought of teaching a Sunday school class, donating your time to teach at a homeschool co-op, or writing a blog?

Sharing your knowledge will require something from you, and that sacrifice might be costly. You may feel worn out, dull, or plain old awkward as you stumble to try to find a right fit for this gift to others, but that doesn't mean that your obedience isn't pleasing to God. He doesn't require five-star, Olympic-standard performances. God smiles at our attempts, and your baby steps bring Him delight. You don't need to wait until you know more or are more prepared. You can start being generous with your knowledge right now.

SHIFT IN FOCUS

When you hoard your knowledge, your treasure is internal; you're only thinking of yourself. When you are being generous and sharing your knowledge freely, your heart will be fixed on stewarding what God has given you and bringing glory to Him.

Do you tend to not think you are very knowledgeable or do you lean toward being prideful in how much you know?

What step can you take today to be generous in your knowledge?

DAY 19 • • • • • • • • • •

Greed and Money

As for the rich in this present age, charge them not to be haughty,
nor to set their hopes on the uncertainty of riches, but on God, who
richly provides us with everything to enjoy. They are to do good,
to be rich in good works, to be generous and ready to share, thus
storing up treasure for themselves as a good foundation for the
future, so that they may take hold of that which is truly life.
(1 Timothy 6:17–19)

He who loves money will not be satisfied with money, nor he who
loves wealth with his income; this also is vanity.
(Ecclesiastes 5:10)

Money may bring comfort and security, but it is a poor savior. Money cannot provide you with lasting joy, peace, or salvation. In 1 Timothy, Paul refers to the *"uncertainty of riches,"* and this uncertainty has never changed. People are rich one day and devastatingly poor the next. God is truly in control here, and no amount of money will ensure that God won't overturn your life in His kindness and grace toward your eternal soul.

In Ecclesiastes, Solomon points out the paradox of how money is never truly satisfying and, especially in Western culture, the rich don't even believe they're rich. The people I'm observing in the coffee shop where I'm writing are wearing AirPods and drinking $6 coffees. Studies will show that they are in the top

5 percent of the wealthiest people on earth—but they probably would not say they are rich.

Money can be one of the most tempting things to hoard because it promises comfort, peace, security, protection, and prosperity. But as Jesus tells us in Mark 8:36, *"For what does it profit a man to gain the whole world and forfeit his soul?"*

Godly obedience means having a right view of money. Your money is not yours. It is a gift from God that He has entrusted you to steward. Someday you'll be asked by Him how well you stewarded your money. God tells us in Scripture that we are to be generous, giving from our abundance, and we are to tithe and take care of the shepherds pouring their lives out for God's people. But, ultimately, we are to view our money as God's and obey His will for allocating it.

SHIFT IN FOCUS

Only you and God can truly work out how God would have you spend, save, and tithe your money, but it's a good practice to bring your money to God often and let Him check your heart and loosen your grip on what is not truly yours.

Do you trust Him to do that work in your life? Do you trust that God can take care of you, even if you do not have an ample savings account?

DAY 20 • • • • • • • • • • •

Living with Hands and Heart Open
By Alison Bradley

Oh, fear the LORD, you his saints, for those who fear him have no lack! The young lions suffer want and hunger; but those who seek the LORD lack no good thing.
(Psalm 34:9–10)

I think that greed is a symptom of believing the lie that there won't be enough. And the belief that there won't be enough strikes my heart at all sorts of moments. It can strike when I'm grocery shopping and I'm struck by a desire to stock up on everything I could ever need. It can strike when I'm writing and I'm tempted to hold back and "save" ideas in case I run out of them.

One year for Lent, the Lord asked me to fast stinginess and replace it with generosity. That began a journey with the Lord of opening my eyes to what generous living really looks like. I often had to name the fear and scarcity I was believing—*the Lord will stop providing, and I have to do it all on my own*—and replace it with the act of trusting in the abundance of the Lord. It meant replacing my posture of tightly clenched fists with surrendered, open hands.

I think our specifics will look different, especially in different seasons. But opening my hands means I trust the Lord to care for me. I'm exercising a real, practical, everyday trust in the Lord to take care of me. I'm noticing when scarcity strikes my heart and when I fear the Lord won't come through for me. I'm shifting my focus from my fears of "not enough" to who the Lord is. I'm preaching the truth to my own heart about the character of God. I'm reminding myself about the ways I've already experienced His abundance and generosity in my own story.

SHIFT IN FOCUS

I invite you to pick one of the following practices in order to move toward living with your hands open today. The Lord doesn't want you to live in fear or scarcity, dear Five. His generous heart invites you to believe the truth of His abundant love for you.

+ Meditate on Psalm 16 or Psalm 34. Consider picking a verse to memorize. What do you notice about the Lord's provision and generosity here? What truth does your heart need to hear today?

+ Make a gratitude list. How have you experienced the Lord's goodness this week?

+ Read Joshua 5:12: *"And the manna ceased the day after they ate of the produce of the land."* Sometimes the Lord's provision might look different, but the heart of the Giver remains the same. Can you think of a time when the Lord took care of you in a way that was different than you expected?

+ Close your eyes and make your hands into fists. Ask the Lord what you need to release to Him today. Think of one or two things to surrender to Him. Open your hands and imagine releasing that thing to Him. Now, cup your hands and ask Him what gift He might have for you today.

+ Remember a time you experienced the Lord's abundant, personal care for you. Spend a few minutes remembering what happened, perhaps journaling about what you can recall. Thank the Lord for His goodness to you in the past, and invite Him to help you trust Him to continue to provide for all you need.

10 DAYS OF OBJECTIVITY

Your Strength and How to Use It to the Glory of God

● ● ● ● ● ● ● ● ● ● ● **DAY 21**

What Is Objectivity?

> *For the LORD your God is God of gods and Lord of lords,*
> *the great, the mighty, and the awesome God,*
> *who is not partial and takes no bribe.*
> (Deuteronomy 10:17)

When we talk about Fives and how they're objective, we mean they're often not influenced by personal feelings, interpretations, or prejudice. They can make decisions based on facts and remain unbiased. They can separate their thoughts from their personal feelings, and they're able to see the big picture instead of being paralyzed by the feelings at hand. Obviously, this is not true 100 percent of the time, or for all Fives, but, in general, objectivity is considered a strength of Enneagram Fives.

Being objective is a good thing when you're needing to make big decisions and bias or emotions are high. This is why people often recruit someone who is unbiased or not emotionally involved in the situation to give them advice. They can trust this objective party to look at the facts and give them good advice.

For example, you may be offered a new job very far away from where you live currently. The adventure of moving, the pay raise, and the new title are alluring, but it would mean moving away from your parents, your kid's current school, and everything you've ever known.

Being objective would help you weigh this situation for the good of your family and listen to what God might be telling you instead of what your loud emotions are shouting.

In the end, either staying or moving could be the right choice, but making an objective decision can be key to making a decision you won't later regret—and one you can have peace in making.

SHIFT IN FOCUS

Have you ever been called objective?

Do you tend to see this as a strength?

It can be encouraging to see objectivity as a strength when a lot of people probably see your ability to take emotion out of the equation to be a flaw. However, in verses like Deuteronomy 10:17 we see that God Himself is unbiased, doesn't play favorites, and takes no bribes.

● ● ● ● ● ● ● ● ● ● **DAY 22**

Objectivity and Emotion

Ponder the path of your feet; then all your ways will be sure.
(Proverbs 4:26)

Those of us who are not Fives think of objectivity as logical thinking or being unemotional. But it's more than that. Objective thinking is not about having no emotions or biases—it's knowing when to listen to them and when not to.

As a Four myself, I struggle to understand this, but I can't help but be in awe of this ability in Fives. Learning about the Enneagram has helped me understand Fives in a much deeper way than what I would've assumed by observation. Dear Five, your ability to set aside emotion is not a sign of your lack of emotions. Fives are deep people who love connection and have a vivid inner world. You have feelings (inside impression) but don't always express them as emotion (outside expression) in ways the rest of us recognize.

My dad is very likely a Five, and his love looks a lot like giving advice, fixing things when they're broken, and dropping anything to come jump-start my car on his day off. My dad may not cry, rage, or be overly mushy in his expression of emotion. But I can feel his love loud and clear.

As a Five, your emotional expression might look different than other people's in some ways, but your emotions are still alive and well inside you.

In emotion, a lot of us say things we don't mean. In emotion, a lot of us hit first and ask questions later. In emotion, a lot of us make big decisions that outlast what we felt while making them. But in objectivity, Fives ponder their path and take steps accordingly—even when it's a hard decision emotionally.

SHIFT IN FOCUS

Have you ever thought of the difference between emotion and feelings?

This week, communicate what this difference is to someone in your life, and detail to them how you express emotion in ways they may not recognize.

• • • • • • • • • • • **DAY 23**

An Objective God

*Knowing that whatever good anyone does, this he will receive back
from the Lord, whether he is a bondservant or is free.
Masters, do the same to them, and stop your threatening,
knowing that he who is both their Master and yours is in heaven,
and that there is no partiality with him.*
(Ephesians 6:8–9)

*Now then, let the fear of the LORD be upon you. Be careful what
you do, for there is no injustice with the LORD our God,
or partiality or taking bribes.*
(2 Chronicles 19:7)

We serve an objective, unbiased, and fair God, which is great news for us. God does not create us on unequal footing with regard to Himself; we are all deeply loved, and He died for us all. (See 2 Corinthians 5:15.)

In Ephesians 6, Paul is writing to masters about their treatment of their slaves. The context of slavery can rightfully make us uncomfortable, but unfortunately, this discomfort can distract from the beautiful truth found in these guidelines. *"He who is both their Master and yours is in heaven, and that there is no partiality with him"* (Ephesians 6:9). There is no favoritism in God. He doesn't regard wealth, beauty, or fame. He created us all, and that's where our worth lies. *"All things were created through him and for him"* (Colossians 1:16).

As an Enneagram Five, you reflect this beautiful nature of God. We know how hard it is to be truly unbiased as humans, and even you as a Five are not completely free of bias, prejudice, or privilege. However, your ability to lay aside emotion when needed is a reflection of God's perfect, unbiased character.

When others see you put truth before feeling, choose something that's right instead of something that serves you, or give objective advice, they're experiencing the just nature of God, and this brings glory to Him.

Sometimes people may not view your objective thinking as kind, but we don't always understand the kindness of God until after the fact either. Your family and close friends might especially be taken aback when you are not completely biased in their favor, but that doesn't mean you need to remain silent. We need your voice, we need your thoughts, and we need your reflection of God here.

SHIFT IN FOCUS

What's a situation you didn't think was for your good at the time, but looking back, you wouldn't change a thing?

How does reflecting God's objective thinking encourage and challenge you?

• • • • • • • • • • • DAY 24

The Bible and Objective Thinking

*And all Israel heard of the judgment that the king had rendered,
and they stood in awe of the king, because they perceived that the
wisdom of God was in him to do justice.*
(1 Kings 3:28)

We talked about Solomon on Day 6, and today we are back
to inspect one part of his story. First Kings 3 is set around
three years after King David's death, and about one year before
Solomon would start building the temple. This story was the cat-
alyst for Solomon's wisdom becoming legendary—and it was all
because of this tale of objective thinking at its finest.

The tale goes like this: two women came to Solomon to settle
a dispute. It was common for people to bring matters to the king
in this way, but this dispute was serious. Both of these women
had newborn sons, and one of the infants had died in the middle
of the night. Now both women were claiming the living newborn
as their own. There was no such thing as a DNA test in those
days, and these women were prostitutes, so the fathers of these
children were likely unknown or nowhere to be found. Solomon
would have been raised to look down on these women because of
their lifestyle and gender. Thus, he wouldn't have been motivated
to spend much time or energy getting to the truth of the matter.
This attitude is apparently what we see from him at first: he said,
*"Divide the living child in two, and give half to the one and half to the
other"* (verse 25). At this, one of the women became distraught

and said, *"Oh, my lord, give her the living child, and by no means put him to death"* (1 Kings 3:26), while her counterpart has no qualms about the baby being cut apart.

Solomon took his own prejudice and emotion out of the situation and in doing so revealed the truth. The woman who did not want the child to be killed was the true mother. Solomon was wise enough to be sly and objective enough not to get too wrapped up in the women's emotions or his preconceived ideas about them.

We see from 1 Kings 3:28 that this story brought glory not only to Solomon but to God. The people of Israel knew that the wisdom of God was in Solomon because this wisdom could not have come from man. This type of wisdom can't be taught. As a Five, you have this same gifting in you—not just because of your objective nature, but because you have the same God as Solomon.

SHIFT IN FOCUS

Pause and read 1 Kings 3:16–28.

Were you familiar with this story?

What is one new thought you had about this story after rereading it?

• • • • • • • • • • • DAY 25

Objectivity in Cultural Narratives

The saying is trustworthy and deserving of full acceptance,
that Christ Jesus came into the world to save sinners,
of whom I am the foremost.
(1 Timothy 1:15)

One of the topics you might run across if you Google search "objective thinking" is "Can history be told objectively?" Can we somehow sift through stories told on a bias and come out with objective truth?

This is a conundrum for a species so entrenched in sin as ours. We are selfish, we seek our own gain, and when we tell the stories we are involved in, we tend to tell them in a flattering light. It takes humility to openly share facts that may paint yourself in a negative light. We see this kind of humility in the apostle Paul's writing. He didn't shy away from speaking of himself as "the worst of sinners" and speaking of his sin in the present tense.

He explains that he does this because when he, in his weakness and as a sinner needing a Savior, did anything of note, anything worthy of praise, or anything life changing, Christ was all the more glorified. Paul tells the story of his ministry and his past in humility and truth.

As you read about history, or even experience our current climate, you might find it frustrating to try to find truth through all the noise. Part of this frustration lies in your gifting of objectivity. If history were only told by Fives, we'd probably have a better, clearer picture of what has happened.

I find that the areas we are most gifted in are often our frustration points with others. If something is easy for you, then when it's not easy for someone else, it feels like they're choosing not to do something simple.

This area of objective storytelling can be an area where you lend your gifting to the narrative, but it can also be an opportunity for growth and patience while you understand that not everyone has your abilities.

SHIFT IN FOCUS

Can you see how Fives' gifts of objective thinking help the entire world understand our history?

Are you often frustrated by those who don't think objectively? What does patience look like here?

• • • • • • • • • • • • **DAY 26**

Tips for Giving Advice
By Jarrett Bradley

A woman from Samaria came to draw water. Jesus said to her,
"Give me a drink." (For his disciples had gone away into the city to
buy food.) The Samaritan woman said to him, "How is it that you,
a Jew, ask for a drink from me, a woman of Samaria?" (For Jews
have no dealings with Samaritans.)
(John 4:7–9)

In John 4, we find the recounting of Jesus speaking to a Samaritan woman at a well. The interaction between the two individuals is utterly fascinating, especially when considering the social status of each. Among the Jews in the ancient Near East, men were considered higher in social status than women, and rabbis were held in even greater esteem. Conversely, to be a woman was considered lowly. To be born of Samaritan descent was worse. The status of the woman to whom Jesus spoke was worse still because she had been with multiple men throughout her life. This woman, by social reckoning, was at the very bottom of the social ladder.

Jesus shows tremendous compassion for her in their conversation, but what's equally important is what He does *not* say. Imagine being in Jesus's position and speaking to someone whom society considers an utter and complete failure. You have all the cards, and you have all the answers. Why not tell this woman to get her life together? "Stop sleeping around! Repent of what you've done! Stop avoiding the question of where you can and can't worship and just worship God! Get it together!" And yet, when Jesus interacted with the Samaritan woman, He said none of these things, even though He could have, better than anyone.

For us, advice giving, as it is generally experienced, fails to acknowledge the human heart. It takes perceived information, grinds it up, and spits out "advice" that is neither appetizing nor wholesome. Telling the woman at the well to "get her act together" certainly would not have changed her heart, and chances are she had heard this advice a dozen times already—spoken to her face or otherwise. Advice almost always focuses on external behavior instead of heart change and is, at best, discouraging.

However, Jesus demonstrates for us a different way. He sat with people in pain, He listened, He cared about their problems, and He had the wisdom to know when to be gentle and when to be blunt. Jesus was not interested in pat answers for downcast and suffering people; He was interested in changed hearts.

We too are interested in changed hearts, and the nature of an Enneagram Five lends itself to a rather unique skillset: the ability to objectively listen. In a culture charged with emotion and reactivity, there is a desperate need for individuals who know how to truly listen to the people around them without trying to fix mere externals with advice. Good listening consists of asking questions and working toward understanding. It seeks to sort out the difficulties of life alongside others and is easily one of the greatest services we can offer to those around us.

Jesus had the distinct advantage of being God and knowing everything about the woman at the well, but we have all the tools to understand and love people the way Jesus loved that particular woman. It is up to us, however, to choose to engage the people around us through understanding and leveraging the minds God has given us to serve them in truth and love. People generally cannot receive a logical conclusion if they do not believe that they are first understood.

SHIFT IN FOCUS

Read John 4:1–42.

How does it feel for you when someone gives you advice without context?

What would someone need to believe about themselves and others in order to genuinely enjoy listening to people around them?

DAY 27 • • • • • • • • • • •

Objective Thinking and Close Relationships
By Anna Yates

When they came to the place of which God had told him, Abraham built the altar there and laid the wood in order and bound Isaac his son and laid him on the altar, on top of the wood. Then Abraham reached out his hand and took the knife to slaughter his son. But the angel of the LORD called to him from heaven and said, "Abraham, Abraham!" And he said, "Here I am." He said, "Do not lay your hand on the boy or do anything to him, for now I know that you fear God, seeing you have not withheld your son, your only son, from me." And Abraham lifted up his eyes and looked, and behold, behind him was a ram, caught in a thicket by his horns. And Abraham went and took the ram and offered it up as a burnt offering instead of his son. So Abraham called the name of that place, "The LORD will provide"; as it is said to this day, "On the mount of the LORD it shall be provided."
(Genesis 22:9–14)

I've always thought of myself as quiet and introverted, not a "people person." But the Enneagram showed me how attached I really am to relationships. Even though I'm task-focused and objective, I'm constantly aware of relationships between myself and others and how they affect me.

I calculate how much energy I have to interact with the cashier at the grocery. I sit with one close friend in a small group to feel comfortable in the group dynamics. I prioritize taking a walk with my boyfriend when he visits for family dinner, since that's my one reprieve from draining interactions and my one chance to really connect with him.

When it comes to close relationships, my normally objective mind can become entangled with greedy motives. There's a constant temptation to believe the lie that I am what I have: strong relationships, energy, and "enough." I look to connect with people I love to give me comfort and safety. Getting too attached, I pull away from everyone else and ask the people I love to pull away, too. On the flip side, I fear connections that might cost me too much and withdraw to avoid them.

Dear Five, we need to dig deep and trust God for abundance.

Naturally, I assume over-attachment and hoarding will keep me happy and safe. But really, it's a cycle of fear and isolation that drains me of life, separates me from rewarding though exhausting connections, and alienates me from people I love because they can't be my sole source of happiness. Most of all, it disconnects me from God as my source of life.

The Lord gave me the story of Abraham in Genesis 22 during a time when I was struggling to let go of someone to whom I was dearly attached. Although we were on good terms, it was difficult for me to release what that person meant to me. But God was asking me to release the gift and look to the Giver for life. Regardless of connection or disconnection with others, I'm called to trust that God is enough for me.

Even though lack feels like death for us Fives, it isn't. You will make it. Your well of energy won't stay empty because you're not the one filling it up, and neither are the people who love you. With healthy rhythms of rest and silence, you can dig deeper.

Holding relationships with an open hand lets us relish the gift of connection while maintaining healthy objectivity—objectivity that balances priorities, keeps our focus in the right place, and opens our bodies, hearts, and minds to new possibilities of how God will provide for us.

SHIFT IN FOCUS

Read Genesis 22.

If these words reflect your heart, please borrow them:

Dear heavenly Father, I look to You as the giver of energy, love, and safety. I let go of the fear of lack, of the fear of separation and loneliness, of the lie that I am what I have. I surrender to Your silence. I open my hands and give everything to You. I trust that You are enough for me. Amen.

• • • • • • • • • • **DAY 28**

Objective Thinking and the Workplace

For God is not unjust so as to overlook your work and the love that you have shown for his name in serving the saints, as you still do.
(Hebrews 6:10)

One of the greatest challenges of life is what we do for work, especially for those of us who value work-life balance. Work is a consequence of Adam and Eve's sin, and that's why, even when you're doing something you love, it still feels like work. We all have assets and pain points that follow us to almost any workplace. As a Five, one of your most valuable assets to any employer is your objective thinking.

If you haven't mentioned your objective thinking in a job interview before, I'd encourage you to start using that as one of your strengths. Objective thinking helps you to see the bigger picture, not get easily offended, and make decisions based on facts rather than feelings. Most employers place a high value on objectivity, and it's an area where you are very strong.

Where Fives get into trouble in the workplace is in taking a long time to make decisions, being a little too straightforward, and not always being able to turn on the energy if the situation demands it. You are likely aware of these struggles, and although there is no quick fix for them, just knowing that they exist can make it easier for you to cope with them.

Hebrews 6:10 says that God will not *"overlook your work and the love that you have shown for his name."* When we work as for

God and not for man, and work to love those around us, we are pleasing our heavenly Father.

You can love your coworkers and boss by:

+ Communicating what your workplace boundaries are

+ Engaging in small talk to make them feel comfortable

+ Being upfront and letting them know when you need time to process something

+ Softening your corrections

+ Telling them things about yourself

+ Asserting your worth

SHIFT IN FOCUS

Can you see where objective thinking is helpful in your current job?

Loving your coworkers and boss will feel like "work" in and of itself, but it's work that honors God. What's one thing you could do this week that would be loving to your coworkers and boss?

• • • • • • • • • • • **DAY 29**

Objective Thinking and the Struggle of Faith in the Unknown
By Anna Yates

But now in Christ Jesus you who once were far off have been brought
near by the blood of Christ. For he himself is our peace,
who has made us both one and has broken down in his
flesh the dividing wall of hostility.
(Ephesians 2:13–14)

After I graduated from college, I joined a small congregation called Friendship Church. As is customary for a single girl, I started getting to know one of the single guys at church. Pretty soon, he started sitting next to me every week at service and messaging me regularly on social media. So it wasn't a big surprise when he asked me to dinner after a few months. Our first date was great, and we found out we had a lot more in common than we thought. Afterward, when he called and thanked me for my time, I was disappointed but figured that was the end of it.

The only glitch? We still went to a small church. We were still good friends. He still sought me out at church and during the week since we worked on the same university campus. And it was getting difficult to stay objective.

I didn't understand why this friend had taken romance off the table after the first date. I didn't understand why he was still seeking out deeper friendship. I didn't understand why I couldn't get rid of those pesky feelings. And I didn't understand what

God was doing. I struggled with overthinking and obsessing over the situation.

As a Five, I searched for understanding because I believed it would bring me security. But in the middle of a situation I couldn't figure out no matter how much I thought about it, God gave me Ephesians 2 and the prayer practice of mental silence. Jesus is our peace by breaking down the wall of hostility that separates us from God and from each other. As I meditated on this passage, I saw that presence—not understanding—is the key to peace.

Through mental silence, I worked against overthinking and submitted to God my need to understand. As I released the search for answers, I was able to accept God's presence in a new way. Though I still didn't understand the situation, I found rest and peace for my heart. I relished the moments in the morning when I could quiet my mind, sit with God, and find a brimming well of peace.

Dear Five, you don't have to answer all the questions. You just have to show up in faith.

What are the questions nagging you, the problems distressing you, the burdens weighing you down? It's not your responsibility to answer those questions or solve those problems. God just wants you to show up, be present, and sit in silence with faith He has the answers and He's taking care of you right now, even in the unknown.

SHIFT IN FOCUS

Read Ephesians 2.

Take fifteen minutes today to practice mental silence. Find a quiet, undisturbed corner where you're separated from your responsibilities. Quiet your mind and focus on one word that represents God's presence in your life right now. Turn every other thought away. Feel your breath as God's sustenance and abundant life in you. Sit with God right here, right now.

DAY 30 • • • • • • • • • •

Growing in Godly Objectivity
By Jarrett Bradley

Blessed is the man who trusts in the LORD, whose trust is the LORD.
He is like a tree planted by water, that sends out its roots by the
stream, and does not fear when heat comes, for its leaves remain
green, and is not anxious in the year of drought,
for it does not cease to bear fruit.
(Jeremiah 17:7–8)

What does it mean to have godly objectivity? And how important is such a thing today?

There is a sense in which the term "godly objectivity" sounds stiff and dated—something stuffy pastors used one hundred years ago but which we modern people have moved on from. If that happens to be the case, then what we are probably thinking about is some iteration of legalism, which has always sprouted up in the church. However, godly objectivity is not legalism; it is far more dynamic, beautiful, and alive than legalism could ever hope to be; ultimately, it brings us freedom because it also involves trust.

What is godly objectivity then? It is the discipline, practice, and integration of seeing the world, ourselves, and others the way that God sees them. God is the one who brought everything that exists into actuality, which means that there is no other entity who better understands the nature of literally everything, or the means by which to let creation, in all of its aspects, thrive. That includes you and me.

When God speaks through the prophet Jeremiah, it is we who can be like the tree planted by water, who does not worry when a temporary drought passes in the land. To see the world in the way that God sees it—to have godly objectivity—does not merely give us tools to approach life in the best way possible (though it does that as well), but, if we allow it, it also nourishes our soul to the point that we can become the person God ultimately created us to be.

The trouble resides in allowing God's truth to enter us and then change us. We are so frequently bombarded with ideas about being "true to ourselves" and "following our heart" that the idea of allowing an outside entity to *change* us can seem downright backwards. However, there is a beautiful—and sometimes vexing!—paradox at play when it comes to God and His kingdom. To allow yourself to "lose" your "self" to God is to become fully true to yourself. It is the kind of individual self that our culture longs for but can never attain because to get there involves doing precisely the opposite of what one would expect. To find freedom in who we are, we must become a willing slave to the One who created us.

Becoming a slave to God and His truth as we grow in godly objectivity brings us freedom in our innermost being and, incidentally, gives us tremendous insight into how to operate in God's creation. However, to do so is also a practice, something that must be done intentionally. It takes time to learn from God, our teacher, and to attune our hearts and minds to the Holy Spirit.

But the final result is freedom, real freedom, the kind where we really can do whatever we want because when our hearts are attuned to God's, even our clumsiest, stumbling efforts will naturally sprout goodness.

SHIFT IN FOCUS

Are there areas in your life where you are currently feeling anxious?

How are you putting your trust in that area? Is there an aspect of God's truth that could replace that trust?

Take some time to talk to the Holy Spirit about those things, thinking of Him as a friend sitting next to you. See if there is anything He wishes to say to your heart, or if He simply wants to listen to you.

10 DAYS OF LOW ENERGY
Help with a Common Pain Point

• • • • • • • • • • • DAY 31

Are All Fives Introverts?

Be still, and know that I am God. I will be exalted among the
nations, I will be exalted in the earth!
(Psalm 46:10)

One of the most obvious personality differences between people is energy level. Especially in Western culture, we tend to fixate on the idea of introverts and extroverts as a way to explain ourselves. Although these are helpful distinctions, they just touch the surface of who we are.

Being an introvert means you gain energy from being alone and tend to go inward to experience life. Being an extrovert means you gain energy from being around others and go externally to experience life. You can be quiet and be an extrovert, and you can be loud and be an introvert, because these distinctions are not about behaviors as much as they are about how you gain energy.

One of the ways you can tell which you are is by asking yourself how you feel after being in a large group of people. My husband and I are both introverted, and we become very tired—and barely talkative, even with each other—after being around large numbers of people. I've heard the extroverts in my life talk about feeling buzzed, and almost having a hard time calming down, after a long period of socializing. As an introvert, I run out of energy after socializing, but an extrovert has more energy than that cute pink bunny who runs on batteries.

The truth is, *most* Fives are introverts and Fives are believed to have the smallest amount of social energy on the Enneagram. If you are an extrovert and a Five, you'll feel a lot of tension in your life because you'll need people to energize you...but you'll also feel a need to take a break from people. As much as people can invigorate you, it takes a lot of work to get to a comfort level where that fortification happens. Perhaps a couple of people in your life energize you and you don't like being alone, yet big groups of people can still feel draining. Even if you can be loud and appear outgoing in public, if you are drained when you get home, you're introverted.

This is one of the most beautiful and frustrating things about the Enneagram: it's fluid enough that almost any behavior is possible as long as your core motivation is on point. So instead of asking, "Are all Five introverts?" I ask myself, "Why would a Five be an extrovert? How would that look?"

The Enneagram is a framework, and that's why questions like, "Is (fill in the blank) normal?" or "Do Fives always behave like (fill in the blank)?" will always be met with: "It depends."

You don't have to second guess your Enneagram typing just because everything written about your type isn't on point. You are able to be your personal version of Five-ness, still motivated by competency but working that out in your own way.

SHIFT IN FOCUS

Where do you find yourself on the introvert vs. extrovert scale?

Do you feel like you're obviously an introvert or an extrovert in public?

Is it part of your nature to "be still," or do you find that hard?

DAY 32 • • • • • • • • • • •
Low Social Energy

And he answered, "You shall love the Lord your God with all your heart and with all your soul and with all your strength and with all your mind, and your neighbor as yourself."
(Luke 10:27)

What does a Five's low social energy look like in practice?

The amount of energy you woke up with this morning is being depleted all day long. Once it's gone, it's time to rest and replenish it.

Now, there are different kinds of energy: mental energy, emotional energy, and physical energy, just to name a few. Fives do pretty well with mental and physical energy, but struggle with emotional or social energy. You may have enough physical energy for an event, but emotionally, you know it will be hard on you. You may mentally be up for a conversation about a topic that interests you, but hearing someone's life story interjected into the conversation may cause you to retreat inward and tune out.

As a Five, you are a doer. You have energy to accomplish whatever is required, but usually not for all the social fluff that others make you go through to spend time with them.

This means that you are probably pretty selective about the events you attend. You may leave early. Perhaps you're relieved when plans are canceled. You may force yourself to go to a social function that you would rather skip just to appease someone, only to be only half there because you don't have the energy to give other people or the occasion your full attention.

If this is you, may I give you permission to set up some boundaries here? You can take a separate car, you can say no, or you can explain to those closest to you about your limited social energy and give them your clues for "I need to leave now."

The people who love you don't want you to be miserable or force you to do something you're not up for because that doesn't actually serve them. They'll be constantly wishing you were having a good time when you're just not. You can help them have a good time by letting them know they don't have to worry about you. You'll be happy at home or you'll let them know when you need to go. Either way, it's a win-win for you both.

SHIFT IN FOCUS

In your day-to-day life, can you spot the difference between your mental, emotional, and physical energy?

What boundaries do you need to put up around your social energy?

What's one action step you can take toward putting up boundaries today?

DAY 33 • • • • • • • • • •

Living with an Obvious Deficiency

For to one is given through the Spirit the utterance of wisdom, and to another the utterance of knowledge according to the same Spirit, to another faith by the same Spirit, to another gifts of healing by the one Spirit, to another the working of miracles, to another prophecy, to another the ability to distinguish between spirits, to another various kinds of tongues, to another the interpretation of tongues. All these are empowered by one and the same Spirit, who apportions to each one individually as he wills.
(1 Corinthians 12:8–11)

I'm sure you've heard more than your fair share of questions like these:

+   Why are you so quiet?

+   You know it's okay to talk, right?

+   You can speak up; we don't bite.

+   You look like you're off in space!

These words and other people's general demeanor toward you might make you feel like you're living with an obvious deficiency that you can't hide. So you hide yourself or you learn not to care.

Many Fives aren't even necessarily quiet people but have probably still heard these comments from time to time. Fives like to observe, and it can take a little time for them to feel comfortable in a new environment, which leads to people seeing Fives as quiet, standoffish, or withdrawn.

Although you may not get hurt by what people think of you—especially if they're strangers—you may feel annoyed and anything but complimented by these observations.

You may feel like low energy is a fatal flaw and one that's difficult to hide. You may know comments are coming before they do but can't even muster up enough energy to care, thinking, *It is what it is.*

There is nothing wrong with you. God didn't create you with "less" just for kicks. God created you with a unique purpose and unique skills, just like He created others with a unique purpose and unique skills. No one's skill or purpose is greater than that of their neighbors; they're just different. And as we see in 1 Corinthians, *"All these are empowered by one and the same Spirit, who apportions to each one individually as he wills."*

Maybe you know this and you already appreciate the gifts that God has given you. But when the world praises certain gifts and sees others as "less than" or unworthy of respect, you can't hear the truth too much.

SHIFT IN FOCUS

How do you feel when others tell you you're quiet?

How do you remind yourself of the truth of your gifts?

DAY 34 • • • • • • • • • • •

You Were Created Purposefully
By Alison Bradley

But now thus says the LORD, he who created you, O Jacob, he who formed you, O Israel: "Fear not for I have redeemed you; I have called you by name, you are mine. When you pass through the waters, I will be with you; and through the rivers, they shall not overwhelm you; when you walk through fire you shall not be burned, and the flame shall not consume you."
(Isaiah 43:1–2)

It is easy enough to believe in our heads that the Lord made us with intention. If you grew up in church or watched *VeggieTales*, you probably heard as a child that "God made you special." But even if you didn't, that knowledge has probably made it into your head at some point. But has it reached your heart? What does it mean for you now that God made you special?

I invite you to return to today's verses and insert your own name instead of the names of Jacob and Israel as you reread them. You were created by the Lord, dear Five. The Lord formed you with your specific strengths and personality. Verse 4 in this same passage of Scripture speaks to the love and tenderness the Lord holds for you, His child: *"You are precious in my eyes, and honored, and I love you."* It may be hard to hold that truth in tension with the parts of yourself that don't feel quite as desirable, like having less energy than most people. Yet, I think it shifts something in my heart to know the intention and love behind my personality and body being made by God Himself. Even if I have a hard time appreciating something about myself, it helps me reframe it to know the Lord made me with intention and delights in me.

This passage doesn't simply remind us of how the Lord made each of us. The belief that we are lovingly formed is the foundation for believing that we don't have to fear when things feel overwhelming or too much for us. Like a loving parent, the Lord goes with us when things are scary. When we feel like we might drown, the Lord does not leave us alone. I can't help but believe these verses don't just speak to physical dangers, but also to times of depletion, weakness, and even low energy.

SHIFT IN FOCUS

Take a few minutes to read the following verses from Psalm 139, aloud if you are able, pausing to invite the Lord to help you listen well to His voice as you read. Think of what parts of yourself are harder to accept as "wonderful." Name those things and invite the Lord to help you believe the truth of these verses.

For you formed my inward parts; you knitted me together in my mother's womb. I praise you, for I am fearfully and wonderfully made. Wonderful are your works; my soul knows it very well. My frame was not hidden from you, when I was being made in secret, intricately woven in the depths of the earth. Your eyes saw my unformed substance; in your book were written, every one of them, the days that were formed for me, when as yet there was none of them.

(Psalm 139:13–16)

DAY 35 • • • • • • • • • • •

Jesus Stewarded His Energy
By Alison Bradley

And he said to them, "Come away by yourselves to a desolate place
and rest a while." For many were coming and going,
and they had no leisure even to eat. And they went away in
the boat to a desolate place by themselves.
(Mark 6:31–32)

In the midst of accounts of teaching and healing, parable deliveries and miracles, we find a few verses tucked throughout the Gospels that speak to how Jesus was able to do all that He did: He stewarded His energy. After Mark records the death of John the Baptist and the sending out of the twelve apostles, he offers the story of Jesus feeding the five thousand (Mark 6). But before that miracle takes place, wedged between the busyness of ministry and grief, we find Jesus noticing the need for rest and taking the time to be alone. He invites His disciples to join Him in this rest. They set out in a boat to find a place to be alone.

But their rest doesn't last for long. Mark tells us that many people recognize Jesus and run ahead of Him so that when the boat gets to shore, there is already a great crowd gathered. I'm touched by Jesus's compassion when His rest doesn't turn out the way He had hoped. Instead of expressing resentment or irritation that He didn't get to rest the way He intended, He has compassion for those who are eager to be taught and cared for by Him.

But the story doesn't end there. It can be easy to be distracted by the breaks that translators have placed in our Bibles, but we're told Jesus teaches until it grows late and then feeds the crowds through the miracle of multiplying the five loaves and two fish to feed everyone until they are satisfied.

Notice how Jesus again recognizes His need for rest as soon as the leftovers are collected: *"Immediately he made his disciples get into the boat and go before him to the other side, to Bethsaida, while he dismissed the crowd. And after he had taken leave of them, he went up on the mountain to pray"* (Mark 6:45–46). While Scripture doesn't tell us directly, we can assume that Jesus was listening to His needs and noticing the needs of His disciples. He didn't wait to see if there were more needs in the crowd of people (I'm sure there were) or if He was still wanted (I'm sure He was). He didn't wait for permission to rest but created the space to get away. He also helps His disciples get away as soon as possible and takes the time to be truly alone by Himself to pray.

SHIFT IN FOCUS

Hebrews 4:15 reminds us, *"We do not have a high priest who is unable to sympathize with our weaknesses, but one who in every respect has been tempted as we are, yet without sin."*

How does it feel to see that Jesus knows what it is like to have His energy stores depleted?

If you have time, I encourage you to read Mark 6 for yourself, paying attention to what Jesus models for us about stewarding His energy.

He modeled for us that sometimes we need to get away alone and sometimes we can rest with others who are safe for us. Jesus also modeled compassion toward those who interrupted Him when rest didn't go the way He hoped. He modeled for us that it is okay to listen to our needs and create space for rest.

Pause to thank Jesus for His example, for how He is able to sympathize when your energy stores run out. Is anything stirring up in you as you read today's reading? If so, I invite you to tell Jesus about it.

● ● ● ● ● ● ● ● ● ● ● **DAY 36**

What the Bible Says about Energy and Rest
By Alison Bradley

Have you not known? Have you not heard? The LORD is the everlasting God, the Creator of the ends of the earth. He does not faint or grow weary; his understanding is unsearchable. He gives power to the faint, and to him who has no might he increases strength. Even youths shall faint and be weary, and young men shall fall exhausted; but they who wait for the LORD shall renew their strength; they shall mount up with wings like eagles; they shall run and not be weary; they shall walk and not faint.
(Isaiah 40:28–31)

It can be easy to believe the lie that you are what you do. This is a tempting lie not only when you are accomplishing a great deal, but also when you don't have much to offer. When you don't have much energy or feel empty, it can feel defeating and discouraging to feel less-than, incompetent, or not as good as someone who can do more. When you feel depleted, it can be a challenge to receive true rest and refilling and believe the truth that we are loved apart from what we do.

I love how Scripture invites us to believe the truth for when we are empty and our energy runs low. Isaiah 40:28–31 might be a familiar passage for you, but I invite you to slow down and notice what it says about rest. Ask the Lord to help your heart listen as you read these verses.

This passage begins by grounding us in who the Lord is. He is the Creator of the ends of the earth. There is no end to His energy, ability, or wisdom. And we find the generosity of the Lord so apparent in these verses. He willingly shares His strength and understanding with those who are weary and weak. He gives freely of what He has in abundance to those who have true need of His strength.

There is so much permission in these verses to notice when you are depleted and feel no shame for it. Even those in their youthful prime become tired and exhausted. These verses tell us that running out of energy and strength is part of being human. Even the strongest and youngest will grow weary. There are times when even those with the most stamina and abilities feel drained and empty.

These verses end with an invitation and an incredible image of what it is like when the Lord shares His strength with us. We are invited to wait on the Lord, trusting that He deeply loves us even when we have nothing to offer Him. And when we do, we will fly like the majestic eagle and run any race set before us.

SHIFT IN FOCUS

Do you find it easy to believe the lie that *you are what you do?*

When you have your energy depleted, is it hard to believe that you are as loved as when you are productive?

Does it feel hard to accept that being tired and empty is part of being human?

Spend a moment to examine your own heart with the Lord as you answer these questions. Invite Him to help you hold onto the truth that you are loved whether you are tired and depleted or strong and energetic. Is there anything you want to thank Him for as you respond to these verses?

Go deeper by spending a few moments meditating on these Scripture readings:

> *And he said, "My presence will go with you, and I will give you rest."* (Exodus 33:14)

> *I lay down and slept; I woke again, for the LORD sustained me.* (Psalm 3:5)

> *For I will satisfy the weary soul, and every languishing soul I will replenish.* (Jeremiah 31:25)

DAY 37 • • • • • • • • • •

Trusting God to Refill You
By Alison Bradley

Blessed be the Lord, who daily bears us up; God is our salvation. Selah. Our God is a God of salvation, and to GOD, the Lord, belong deliverances from death.
(Psalm 68:19–20)

When our energy is low, it can be a challenge to trust that the Lord will fill up our empty tank.

David, in Psalm 25:1–3 models for us what it can look like to come to the Lord when we're feeling drained. Pause and read his words:

> *To you, O LORD, I lift up my soul. O my God, in you I trust; let me not be put to shame; let not my enemies exult over me. Indeed, none who wait for you shall be put to shame.*

I love that we can sense David's struggle to connect this truth from his head down to his heart, even as he is declaring it is true. He's asking the Lord to not let him be put to shame, even as he says he knows that those who wait on the Lord never are.

When we invite the Lord into our everyday struggles, we get to show up as David did. We say, "To You, O Lord, I lift up my soul, and in You I trust," as we ask for His strength to make it through the rest of our workday. We ask Him to help us not be put to shame as we ask for His help to know what to make for dinner that matches our energy level, our pantry shelves, and what we have in the fridge. This isn't abstract head knowledge. We have access to real, tangible help from the Lord when we are running empty. It may feel silly or appear naive to trust the Lord, but we exercise our trust every time we invite the Lord to help us where we are weak. We open our hands to receive the Lord's goodness and provision as we wait for Him, naming our need and inviting Him to care for us.

SHIFT IN FOCUS

Blessed be the Lord, who daily bears us up....Our God is a God of salvation, and to GOD, the Lord, belong deliverances from death. (Psalm 68:19–20)

This Scripture offers the incredible truth that the same God who can bring dead things back to life and do the mightiest of miracles is also personal enough and gentle enough to meet us in our daily struggles.

Where do you need the Lord to refill you today?

What daily needs do you have this very day, this very week?

Pause and make a list, whether mentally or in writing. Bring your list to the Lord, inviting Him to help you trust Him to provide for your energy needs here. Thank Him for being the God of daily life, the God who never lets those who trust in Him be put to shame.

DAY 38 • • • • • • • • • • •

Living with a Low Battery in American Culture

Then I considered all that my hands had done and the toil I had expended in doing it, and behold, all was vanity and a striving after wind, and there was nothing to be gained under the sun. (Ecclesiastes 2:11)

I don't think I've ever heard a Five say that they *enjoy* having low energy. It's just a fact, something that's woven into their everyday life that they work around. Being low energy, quiet, or introverted is not the American ideal. If anything, we live in a Three's world, where social prowess, confidence, and extroversion are praised.

We are the land of fame, fortune, and opportunity. We never have enough, we chase success, and we post about everything we do on some sort of social media platform. We assume others want our opinion before they ask for it, and productivity is why you're still alive. This is America; who needs sleep anyway?

In 2019, *The Washington Post* claimed that 55 percent of Americans don't use all of their paid vacation time every year. You can't even get us to stop running on our hamster wheel if you pay us!

I don't know about you, but I'm exhausted just reading all of this. No wonder we who have lower social energy, value work-life balance, and enjoy a slower pace of life tend to think something is wrong with us. We can't keep up, we weren't built to, and we shouldn't have to.

In the book of Ecclesiastes, Solomon mentions time and time again about *"striving after wind."* This elusive peace, happiness, self-worth, and comfort is what we chase, and we can never quite grasp it.

This is because we were not made for earth to be our home. This life, if you're a Christian, is the closest to hell that you'll ever be. We are made to be with our heavenly Father, to be right with Him, and to worship Him forever—not to almost kill ourselves striving to make ourselves gods here on earth.

America has a lot of great things to offer us, and I am in no way ungrateful for the freedom we enjoy. But it's good to look at the expectations we all bow to with a critical eye. These expectations make us feel like something is wrong with us, but is there really? Or are we just living in a Three's world?

SHIFT IN FOCUS

Have you ever thought about your culture not being made for you?

Take a moment to pray for your eyes to be centered on God's purpose for you and not the cultural expectations.

DAY 39 • • • • • • • • • •

Low Battery and Boundaries
By Alison Bradley

Rather, speaking the truth in love, we are to grow up in every way into him who is the head, into Christ.
(Ephesians 4:15)

Dear Five, when your energy tank is low, your instincts about what you need and what boundaries to set in order to get it naturally come out. This is such a good thing! While others can struggle to know what they lack or wonder how to meet their needs, you tend to have a good sense of how to be refilled and what to do about it. This is such a strength of yours.

The shadow side to this strength is the struggle to communicate your needs with those around you. Often, to reserve energy, you will tend to withdraw or pull away, many times without explanation, leaving those who love you confused and hurt about your physical or emotional absence. When you're low on energy, you're more likely to be brief or noncommunicative with the people around you. Even if you're unable to physically remove yourself from a situation, you're likely to begin shutting down emotionally. Please hear that the problem is not with your boundaries. Those are such a strength! The challenge is to communicate your boundaries firmly and lovingly to others when your energy is low.

In Ephesians 4, Paul is talking to the church, speaking about what it means to not be children anymore (verse 14) and to help *"the body grow so that it builds itself up in love"* (verse 16). Paul points to *"speaking the truth in love"* (verse 15) as the primary way we do this. Speaking truthfully and lovingly creates space for the whole body of Christ to be held together, equipped for the work God has for us. Paul says that this is how each member of Christ's body works properly.

Dear Five, your low energy creates a unique opportunity for you to love others. You are able to offer love to those around you when you speak the truth in love about your low energy and what you need. If we take Paul's words to heart, when you speak truthfully and lovingly, you're offering others the chance to grow and be equipped for their own good work. When you communicate your boundaries about taking time alone or not attending a social gathering, this is a way you are loving others. When you say, "My energy is low this week so I'll have to leave early," you're loving well. Not only are you offering others the chance to see you and your needs, but you're inviting others to set and hold good boundaries by your own example.

SHIFT IN FOCUS

What feels challenging to you about communicating to others about your needs or boundaries when your tank is low? As you name that, invite the Lord to help you speak the truth of your needs in love to others. Invite Him to help you love well in this area.

I encourage you, if you have time, to read all of Ephesians 4. As you read, pay attention to any areas of resonance or resistance. What might the Lord be inviting you to do or become today?

DAY 40 • • • • • • • • • •

In Our Weakness, God Is Glorified

I can do all things through him who strengthens me.
(Philippians 4:13)

The Bible talks a lot about our weaknesses as humans. We don't hear "You're the best!" or "You can do it!" in Scripture, although these seem to be the compliments we throw out to each other often—so often, in fact, that they have lost all meaning beyond "stop complaining," "stop doubting," or "stop being anxious."

In Scripture, we hear that we are weak, fickle, and ultimately sinful to our core, which is why Paul says in 2 Corinthians 12:9, *"But he said to me, 'My grace is sufficient for you, for my power is made perfect in weakness.' Therefore I will boast all the more gladly of my weaknesses, so that the power of Christ may rest upon me."*

Because we are weak, God gets all the glory for our strength. If the smallest, weakest kid in your high school class ended up winning *American Ninja Warrior*, you'd be flabbergasted and ultimately chalk it up to some sort of miracle.

This is what happens when sinful, weak, and fickle humans do something selfless, kind, and sacrificial. Nothing about who they are has changed; what has changed is that you're seeing the fruit of the Holy Spirit work within them as a new creation in Christ.

Romans 8:26 says, *"Likewise the Spirit helps us in our weakness. For we do not know what to pray for as we ought, but the Spirit himself intercedes for us with groanings too deep for words."* God will help us in our weakness. He doesn't leave us to flounder without support.

God does not promise that life will be easy, but He does promise that He will be there with us.

When the righteous cry for help, the LORD hears and delivers them out of all their troubles. The LORD is near to the brokenhearted and saves the crushed in spirit. Many are the afflictions of the righteous, but the LORD delivers him out of them all. He keeps all his bones; not one of them is broken.
(Psalm 34:17–20)

He can sympathize with us because Jesus too lived a human life filled with temptation and trials.

For we do not have a high priest who is unable to sympathize with our weaknesses, but one who in every respect has been tempted as we are, yet without sin. Let us then with confidence draw near to the throne of grace, that we may receive mercy and find grace to help in time of need.
(Hebrews 4:15–16)

Even if the world says you don't have what it takes, or you don't have enough energy, confidence, or social grace, Philippians 4:19 tells us, *"And my God will supply every need of yours according to his riches in glory in Christ Jesus."*

This means that if you need to have more energy or social grace in any given situation, God will give you exactly what you need. We may want abundance, but God gives us just enough.

He wants our eyes fixed on Him; He wants us dependent on Him so we don't forget where our "enough" comes from.

SHIFT IN FOCUS

Spend some time in prayer, journaling, or silence reflecting on God's goodness in your weakness.

Go back through your notes from the past nine days and check in with your action steps.

10 DAYS OF BEING SCATTERED
Going to Seven in Stress

• • • • • • • • • • • **DAY 41**

Seasons of Life

For everything there is a season, and a time for every matter under heaven: a time to be born, and a time to die; a time to plant, and a time to pluck up what is planted; a time to kill, and a time to heal; a time to break down, and a time to build up; a time to weep, and a time to laugh; a time to mourn, and a time to dance; a time to cast away stones, and a time to gather stones together; a time to embrace, and a time to refrain from embracing; a time to seek, and a time to lose; a time to keep, and a time to cast away; a time to tear, and a time to sew; a time to keep silence, and a time to speak; a time to love, and a time to hate; a time for war, and a time for peace.
(Ecclesiastes 3:1–8)

In the whirlwind of life, expectations, and demands, it can be hard to think of ourselves as living seasonally. We live on an earth with winter, spring, summer, and fall, and we observe and celebrate the earth and its seasons, but we rarely give ourselves permission to change and transform. Instead, we expect all or nothing. Either I am...or I am not. There is *right now*, and anything worth doing is worth doing *today*. This is especially true in the hustle of America.

Of course, as we look at our own life, seasons are evident. There was that really hard year of illness, there were years of singleness, there were those amazing three months of falling in love, there were years with little kids, there were years of learning—everything in its own season.

We have a lot to learn from the way God created the earth with its seasons. In these verses from Ecclesiastes, Solomon notes there is a season for everything, and we can see that he's talking about us, not just the earth. The wisest king who ever lived says that for every bad or hard season we experience, there is a season of rest and good to come.

SHIFT IN FOCUS

During the next nine days, we will go into detail about what a season of growth looks like for you as a Five.

As you look at your own life today, what season are you in? Read Ecclesiastes 3:1–8 again and pick one or two verbs that represent the season you're currently in.

Are you mourning, or celebrating?

Are you transitioning, or resting?

Are you uprooting, or planting?

If you're in a more hopeful, joyful, and restful season, it may be time to press into growth and celebrate the growth you can see in yourself. If you're in a season of difficulty, transition, and survival, it will be helpful for you to see this time as just a season, and see the hope on the horizon. You may even see some ways that you're growing even in stress and adversity.

Celebrate those wins!

DAY 42 • • • • • • • • • • •

Seasons of Stress

How long must I take counsel in my soul and have sorrow in my heart all the day? How long shall my enemy be exalted over me? Consider and answer me, O LORD my God; light up my eyes, lest I sleep the sleep of death, lest my enemy say, "I have prevailed over him," lest my foes rejoice because I am shaken.
(Psalm 13:2–4)

In light of talking about seasons of life, we have to talk about the seasons of stress we walk through. Some are lighter than others, but all bring the anxiety and feeling of trying to survive that's familiar to us all. These are hard seasons.

When we talk about stress using Enneagram verbiage, we aren't talking about being late for work or losing your keys. We all get frustrated and irritable in those circumstances. No, when the Enneagram refers to stress, it means seasonal stress—you just lost your job, you're transitioning, your loved one just passed, and other harsh and trying circumstances. In those times, you're often in survival mode for months or years. This is the season of stress we are talking about.

A season of stress works like holding a pitcher that fills slowly or quickly, depending on the severity of stress. Once it's filled to the brim, these stress behaviors spill out. You won't be acting out of these behaviors all the time during a stressful season, but you may see a pattern of them spilling out periodically as you try to cope with stress.

For an Enneagram Five, seasons of stress look like picking up the more negative behaviors of an Enneagram Seven. You will not functionally "become" a type Seven, but your normally analytical, reserved, and diligent disposition can take quite the shift during these seasons.

We are going to be going over how this looks practically over the next eight days, so you'll be able to notice these behaviors in your own life and use them as a red flag for dealing with the stress that's causing them.

Seasons of stress can be tricky because we may not even realize we're in them until they're over.

SHIFT IN FOCUS

Do you believe you're currently in a season of stress?

If not, when was the last time you were in a season of stress?

DAY 43 • • • • • • • • • • •

The Struggles of Type Seven

Turn my eyes from looking at worthless things;
and give me life in your ways.
(Psalm 119:37)

A healthy Seven is a bright light and a breath of fresh air to a world in which everyone's eyes are looking down at their phones, only dreaming of the experiences that Sevens make into reality. Contentment is the virtue of a healthy Seven, which makes the sentiment "find joy in the right here, right now" a natural fit for the Seven's already happy disposition.

Average healthy Sevens are going to struggle with *shiny object syndrome*, chasing after fun experiences and things that bring the promise of pleasure. They don't mean to be noncommittal, but to Sevens, there's nothing worse than committing to something and then missing out when something that's a lot more fun comes up. All of these behaviors stem from Sevens' motivation of being satisfied. Chasing after the things they think will satisfy them is a trademark of type Seven.

If you've ever watched the A&E TV show *Intervention*, you'll have seen the many interviews where a family member describes their loved one as a life of the party, happy, and carefree...and expresses bewilderment that their loved one became a drug addict, thief, or prostitute. This is because Sevens have one of the more addictive personalities on the Enneagram—along with

Fours and Sixes—and their impulse-control issues plus pain avoidance create the perfect storm when they're unhealthy.

Why are we talking so much about Sevens in a devotional for Fives? Well, since you go to Seven in stress, learning about this type is essentially learning about yourself—at least a part of yourself. In learning more about Sevens and their tendencies, motivations, and pain, you'll be able to recognize behaviors that come out in stress for you.

Do you notice that, in times of stress, being satisfied becomes more important to you? In what areas do you notice this? Do you feel drawn to excess or experiences that distract you from your stress? Do you become fearful that you'll never be truly satisfied? All of these things can be manifestations of your going to Seven in stress.

In the next several days, we are going to go over several different temptations you may have in stress and explore how to work through them while leaning on God. If you are currently in a season of stress, this content will be helpful but challenging to hear. If you're not in a current season of stress, then it will be useful for you to keep in mind so you can watch out for the red-flag signs of stress.

SHIFT IN FOCUS

Do you have any Sevens in your life?

What do you admire about them?

What is hard for you about them?

DAY 44 • • • • • • • • • •

Red Flags of Stress

Now, therefore, thus says the LORD of hosts: Consider your ways. You have sown much, and harvested little. You eat, but you never have enough; you drink, but you never have your fill. You clothe yourselves, but no one is warm. And he who earns wages does so to put them into a bag with holes.
(Haggai 1:5–6)

One of the most valuable and practical applications from learning your Enneagram type is becoming aware of your stress behaviors. As we mentioned earlier, we are often not aware that we are in a stress season until it's over, but when you start noticing these behaviors, they give you a great opportunity to identify a stress season while you're still in it. This enables you to be more proactive about your stress and also allows you to have grace for yourself and how you're trying to cope.

If you can look back on seasons of stress in your life—or you're currently in such a season—you'll likely see some of these behaviors loud and clear:

- Feeling scattered, like you can't think straight or your thoughts are bouncing from one thing to another.

- Experiencing bursts of hyper-energy.

- Feeling more impulsive.

- Struggling to stay focused

- Feeling lazy and wanting to just zone out.

- Going, going, going...and then crashing.

- Finding it harder to say no to sugar, technology, alcohol, spending, or a myriad of other vices that promise pleasure or numbing.

These behaviors are huge red flags that you're in a season of stress.

Can you feel these in yourself right now? This season, like the ones before, will pass. But acknowledging the season at hand and giving yourself grace for survival will serve you greatly during what can be a very frustrating time.

SHIFT IN FOCUS

In a season of stress you will need relief, but what these Seven-ish behaviors offer you is a false sense of comfort.

When you see these red-flag behaviors popping up in your life, consider taking these steps:

- Ask yourself: what am I stressed about?

- Ask yourself: is there something I can do about this? Consider calling someone close to you, paying a bill, or having a hard conversation with someone.

- If there is nothing you can do, then set a timer for one hour and clean up some area of your home. Do your makeup, or put on something that's not pajamas. Read your Bible and offer up your troubles to God in prayer.

Not all coping mechanisms are bad, but it's necessary to be aware about why you're having to cope and if it's because you're avoiding, numbing, or distracting.

Do you notice yourself avoiding, numbing, or distracting by cleaning? In those times, pray and ask God to remind you to come to His open arms and receive rest.

· · · · · · · · · · · **DAY 45**

The Temptation of Gluttony

But watch yourselves lest your hearts be weighed down with dissipation and drunkenness and cares of this life, and that day come upon you suddenly like a trap.
(Luke 21:34)

One of the temptations that comes with going to Seven in stress is their deadly sin of gluttony. But did you know that gluttony doesn't have to be about food? No, it's much too greedy for your time, money, and affection; gluttony wants to steal your joy and peace in all kinds of ways.

Gluttony is the sin you're indulging in when you use *anything* excessively, without care of consequences, or for a high that numbs you to reality. When you watch TV excessively or without self-control, you're indulging in gluttony. When you go shopping and buy things you can't afford in order to get the high of new things, you are indulging in gluttony. When you sleep in even though you know you'll be rushed or late to work, you're indulging in gluttony. When you know you shouldn't have eaten the whole box of doughnuts or the whole bag of chips, but you've had a hard day and it'll make you feel better, you're indulging in gluttony.

Gluttony seems harmless...until it's not. It's harmless until you lose your job, can't get out from under credit card debt, or can't lose the weight. Sometimes, the gluttonous lapse in self-control leads to bigger and bigger addictions.

We can be addicted to many things, including pain medication, video games, alcohol, and pornography. Abusing anything that can make you forget reality for right now are all at the bottom of the slippery slide of gluttony.

Gluttony is sneaky because it's really good at saying two things:

+ "Just this once."

+ "You deserve this."

God's Word tells urges us to not give in to any temptation to excess because we belong to Him. *"Do you not know that your body is a temple of the Holy Spirit within you, whom you have from God? You are not your own"* (1 Corinthians 6:19).

SHIFT IN FOCUS

How gluttony manifests is as different as each individual Five, but it's one of the easiest temptations to talk yourself into indulging.

Spend some time reflecting on how gluttony might be appearing in your life.

Give three examples:

1. _____

2. _____

3. _____

• • • • • • • • • • **DAY 46**

The Temptation of Laziness

Whatever you do, work heartily, as for the Lord and not for men.
(Colossians 3:23)

The desire of the sluggard kills him, for his hands refuse to labor.
(Proverbs 21:25)

Laziness is a common temptation for Fives in stress and it tends to go hand in hand with gluttony. To be lazy means to be averse or disinclined to work, activity, or exertion. These are the days you don't want to leave the couch, have very little patience for disruption, and get irritated when anything is asked of you.

Laziness can be inaction, but it can also be an attitude. You can physically be working, but when your attitude is lazy, it shows in the quality of your work. The Bible has strong words to say about laziness or "sluggards" in Proverbs, warning that people who indulge in laziness are overall unwise, and will become poor and hungry.

We can surmise from these verses that God hates laziness because it is like a predator that hunts and kills His people. When laziness lays hold of you, you're worshipping comfort over God, who calls you to action, wisdom, and obedience. None of us are impacting others for the glory of God when we are indulging in laziness, and this is precisely why Satan uses it.

The difference between true laziness and purposeful rest is something you're going to have to discern with God, as those boundaries are different for everyone. But when you identify a season of stress, it's fair to be on guard of your heart leaning toward laziness.

Look for irritation.

Look for rest never actually making you feel rested.

Look for a strong aversion toward your job or everyday tasks.

For here, you will find laziness.

SHIFT IN FOCUS

Is your laziness obvious to you or hard for you to pinpoint?

Memorize Colossians 3:23. How does this Scripture change your view of work?

• • • • • • • • • • • **DAY 47**

The Temptation of Self-Comfort
By Alison Bradley

"Ah, stubborn children," declares the LORD, "who carry out a plan but not mine, and who make an alliance, but not of my Spirit, that they may add sin to sin; who set out to go down to Egypt, without asking for my direction, to take refuge in the protection of Pharaoh and to seek shelter in the shadow of Egypt!"
(Isaiah 30:1–2)

When we're in stress, it is so easy to turn to what is familiar and easy for comfort, even if we know it isn't what would be best for us. We certainly aren't alone in the temptation to take control by turning to things that have brought comfort in the past. God's people all through history seem to have struggled with this temptation too.

The Lord speaks to His children who have sought refuge in someone who harmed them in the past. They hadn't asked the Lord for help or direction but went to what was familiar even if it was also harmful. They made a plan for themselves without remembering who they were or their powerful, loving God.

I certainly find myself in these verses, don't you? How quickly I turn to things that have brought me "comfort" in the form of distraction or numbing in the past. I return to familiar comforts even if I know they won't bring the peace or comfort I'm looking for. As I reach for my phone to scroll or lose myself in a show, a book, or a handful of cookies, I forget to seek the Lord and ask Him for help.

What do you seek refuge in? Are there familiar paths of self-comfort you take? Pause and ask the Lord to remind you of the ways you try to create a refuge for yourself apart from Him. Ask for His help to not give into the temptation of familiar self-comfort instead of seeking His help and comfort.

SHIFT IN FOCUS

First Peter 4:12 reminds us not to be surprised by hard times and suffering: *"Beloved, do not be surprised at the fiery trial when it comes upon you to test you, as though something strange were happening to you."* Often, I think our surprise at suffering makes us all the more susceptible to self-comfort. We are caught off guard by pain or difficulty, and we run to what is familiar out of that place.

Peter ends this section of his teaching on suffering with an invitation: *"Let those who suffer according to God's will entrust their souls to a faithful Creator while doing good"* (1 Peter 4:19).

Consider memorizing this verse to help you when the times of stress and suffering come and the temptation to self-comfort is strong.

You're invited to entrust your soul to the Lord. He is faithful. He will help you continue to do good, even in these hard days.

• • • • • • • • • • • DAY 48

Scattered Thinking
By Anna Yates

For now we see in a mirror dimly, but then face to face. Now I know in part; then I shall know fully, even as I have been fully known.
(1 Corinthians 13:12)

A few years ago, my mom started having odd health problems: muscle weakness in her legs, mouth sores, and pain in her sides. In her mid-fifties, she started using a walker. Doctor visits were a cycle of dead ends and references to other specialists.

After months of questions, she received a diagnosis and started platelet treatment through intravenous immunoglobulin (IVIG). But during treatment, everything got worse. For three weeks, Mama was either crying out in pain or in a restless sleep. Several times, I woke up to hear her screaming in the middle of the night.

As the youngest of four children and only girl, I'm really close to my mom. During that time, I felt like I'd lost her, even though she was still alive. I couldn't share stories from school, ask for advice, or just chat. I felt so alone, frightened, and helpless, but I also felt I had to be strong for my dad.

So I turned my energy to what I could control: my senior-level college classes, job, and housework. My mind worked overtime to compensate for how unsafe I felt. I was either 100 percent working or 100 percent avoiding—constantly moving from task to task with no rest, then hiding out and binging on food and TV. This is classic Five stress mode.

Dear Five, you can't answer every question, but you can connect with the One who does.

After those few weeks, things got better. Doctors eventually found the real source of the symptoms: a benign tumor on Mama's spinal cord. They did the surgery, and the Lord's hand was evident throughout the healing process. He was fighting for us. I was helpless to do anything for my mother, but He was working the story to an end that brought honor to His kingdom.

Dear Five, we can't figure out every problem, settle every uncertainty, or avoid pain by numbing it with distractions and quick gratification. There are questions that simply cannot be answered this side of eternity.

I love 1 Corinthians 13:12 because it reminds me that I'm safe in the unknown. Right now, our understanding is painfully lacking. But there's hope: this lack has an end. Until then, God sees with ultimate clarity and fights for us.

Instead of overworking, overthinking, or hiding through distractions, God wants us to stop moving, silence our minds, and let Him do His work. He wants us to trust that He's enough for us. So in the middle of the fear, helplessness, and burdens, let us stand firm, be silent, and see His salvation.

SHIFT IN FOCUS

If these words reflect your heart, please borrow them:

Dear heavenly Father, in the middle of this uncertainty, I choose to silence my mind and trust You. I acknowledge my limitations in understanding and my fear about the future. But I trust that You are keeping me and fighting for me even when I don't see it. I trust that You are making a way for me, even when I don't understand it. I stand still and wait for You. Amen.

DAY 49 • • • • • • • • • •

Finding Comfort in God
By Alison Bradley

But I have calmed and quieted my soul, like a weaned child with its
mother; like a weaned child is my soul within me.
(Psalm 131:2)

What we're seeking in times of stress is comfort, isn't it? We want to be soothed and cared for. So often, we turn to our own limited ability to calm ourselves with things or behaviors that ultimately fail to bring us the comfort we crave so desperately. But like an overtired child who doesn't know what she needs, we don't know what will truly help us. Only the Lord can comfort us in a way that fulfills the desire of our heart when we're stressed or suffering.

In Psalm 131:1–3, David models for us how to receive the Lord's comfort when we are overwhelmed by the circumstances of this world:

> *O Lord, my heart is not lifted up; my eyes are not raised too high; I do not occupy myself with things too great and too marvelous for me.* (Verse 1)

David's posture is a humble one. His eyes aren't looking up. His heart is heavy. Notice how he is choosing not to occupy himself with anything *"too great and too marvelous"* for him. I envision David thinking of the things that weigh heavily on him and giving them to the Lord one by one in prayer. He isn't occupied with things that are beyond his control—not because he isn't burdened by them, but because he has chosen to give them to the Lord.

> *But I have calmed and quieted my soul, like a weaned child*
> *with its mother; like a weaned child is my soul within me.*
>
> (Verse 2)

Even if your own mother wasn't very nurturing, I hope you can imagine what it would be like to be held like David describes. The child David speaks of is weaned; he is not sitting with his mother for nourishment from her milk, but only to receive her comfort. This child is no longer a baby, but is small enough to fit on her lap, perhaps being rocked or sung to. Images are powerful, and I don't think it is an accident that David is sharing this one. He is imagining himself as that child, being soothed by God, receiving the nurturing, calming comfort of being held safely. He has given his burdens to the Lord and is sitting with the Lord now, calmed and quieted.

> *O Israel, hope in the LORD from this time forth and forever-*
> *more.*
>
> (Verse 3)

David ends this short psalm by preaching to himself and those listening to hold tightly to hope. He is reminding himself to hope in the Lord. The Lord is loving and able to hold the weight of all that burdens us. We can trust the Lord with all that is *"too great and too marvelous"* for us.

SHIFT IN FOCUS

I invite you to imitate David and follow the steps of Psalm 131 to receive the Lord's comfort today. What weighs heavy on you? What feels too great for you to bear? I encourage you to list these things and offer them to the Lord in prayer. If it feels helpful, you can imagine yourself handing each thing to the Lord one by one.

Next, imagine yourself being held by the Lord, as David does. What kind of chair are you sitting in? Is the Lord holding you a certain way? Is the Lord speaking to you or singing? Stay with this image as long as it feels helpful.

Lastly, preach to yourself. You can insert your own name into the last verse, "O _____, *hope in the* LORD *from this time forth and forevermore.*"

If you want to go deeper, I encourage you to meditate on Isaiah 51:3 or Psalm 62:8, or listen to the lullaby "La La Lu" by Christy Nockels or any of the songs on her album *Be Held: Lullabies for the Beloved.*

• • • • • • • • • • • DAY 50

Finding Rest in the Midst of Stress
By Alison Bradley

Come to me, all who labor and are heavy laden, and I will give you
rest. Take my yoke upon you, and learn from me, for I am gentle
and lowly in heart, and you will find rest for your souls. For my yoke
is easy, and my burden is light.
(Matthew 11:28–30)

When you are in a season of stress, it is easy for you to want to just pull away from others. In normal circumstances, alone time often recharges you, so it makes sense that you'd try to find respite in it now. I won't deny that a certain amount of alone time can be helpful in stressful times. But what you are truly longing for goes deeper than just needing to recharge alone. You long for rest for your soul when things feel too much and out of your control.

Pause to read the words of Jesus from Matthew 11:28–30, allowing yourself to imagine Jesus saying them to you.

Notice the lack of shaming for being weary or heavy laden. Jesus invites you to rest in Him if these things are true for you. His gentle invitation is for you: "*Come to me.*" He invites you to learn from Him. He is a gentle teacher who wants to help you find true rest for your soul. This invitation to experience true rest is always available to you.

Part of how the Lord often cares for us and offers us rest when we are weary is through other people. Other followers of

Jesus are referred to as "the body of Christ" throughout the New Testament because we actually get to reflect and act like Jesus to each other.

It may be especially tempting to pull away from others and isolate in seasons of stress. If you don't live near those you feel close to or safe with, it will be even easier to withdraw when you're not doing well. But in hard times, you need the rest and comfort that those who know and love you can offer. You need to experience Jesus's gentle love and care when you aren't doing well, and other people are likely to be part of how you will receive the Lord's comfort and rest. We are part of the body of Christ with our fellow believers. With their help and God's grace, our burdens are lightened and shared.

SHIFT IN FOCUS

In these verses from the Gospel of Matthew, Jesus invites you to name when you are weary and heavy laden. I'd like you to consider naming that with someone who is safe to you, allowing yourself to be seen and experience the love of Christ through His body.

Who are the people who have been Jesus to you in the past?

Who is someone in your life with whom you could imagine sharing how you're really doing in a season of stress?

If someone comes to mind, pause to thank the Lord for the gift of this person in your life. Ask the Lord if you need to be seen by them today and give you the courage to pick up the phone, ask to meet them for coffee, or send a text asking for prayer.

If no one comes to mind, I encourage you to begin asking the Lord for a friend like this or the eyes to see someone in your life who might already be safe and willing to love you here.

10 DAYS OF PASSION
Going to Eight in Growth

DAY 51 ● ● ● ● ● ● ● ● ● ●
Seasons of Growth

Every good gift and every perfect gift is from above, coming down from the Father of lights, with whom there is no variation or shadow due to change.
(James 1:17)

As we talked about in the beginning of our conversation about stress, thinking of your life in seasonal terms is not only biblical, but it also gives you a lot more grace and hope for your circumstances. Seasons of stress are the opposite of seasons of growth. The latter are periods in your life in which you feel as if you have room to breathe, have more energy, and can focus on spiritual, mental, and physical growth.

Seasons of growth are often blurry or over-romanticized when we look back at our life as a whole. We either can't remember a time in our life that we didn't feel the hum of anxiety and stress, or we can't live fully in the present because no season will ever be as good as it has been in the past.

Both of these thought processes are unfruitful because they're extremes. There is always a mixture of good and bad in every situation; only the details change. This is a result of living in a fallen world. We are living outside of our natural habitat, and it often feels like a paradox of good and bad at the same time.

Now, this doesn't mean that seasons of stress and growth coexist all the time; often, they don't. Circumstances in our lives often tip the scales. Nothing is ever all bad or all good. Working in a toxic environment or the death of a loved one will send us into a season of stress. Likewise, getting our dream job, hitting a sweet spot with parenting, or flourishing in a good friendship can tip the scale to seasons of growth.

You should push yourself during seasons of growth. Have you been wanting to read a certain book or join a Bible study? Do it! Are you thinking about starting a diet or exercising more? Now's the time! We literally have more mental space, more energy, and more bandwidth when we are in seasons of growth.

We can also see a lot of encouraging behaviors pop up. Press into them and build them in a way that they'll stick beyond this season. Create good habits that will serve a future, stressed-out you. Consistent Bible reading is a must for all of life, but especially those hard days when you feel lost.

Growth seasons are the days of digging deep and reaping the rewards. These seasons are a gift from a heavenly Father who loves you and wants to give you good things.

As we see in 1 Peter 4:10, we should be using these seasons of *good gifts* to not only build up our faith, but also to help others. In the next nine days, you'll see how going to Eight in growth helps you specifically with this.

SHIFT IN FOCUS

Are you currently in a season of growth?

Do you have a couple of good seasons in your past that you might be over-romanticizing, or maybe are ungrateful for?

• • • • • • • • • • • **DAY 52**

What Going to Eight Looks Like

*Let the wise hear and increase in learning, and the one who
understands obtain guidance.*
(Proverbs 1:5)

When we go to our Enneagram growth number during the seasons when we feel our best, we find ourselves growing in ways that may astound us. The strengths and positive aspects of our growth number can take care of many of our worst behaviors.

For Fives, this means growing in passion, asserting yourself, taking action, and feeling more energy. Every time you prioritize something you're passionate about, every time you choose to assert your presence and claim your space, every time you choose action, you're leaning into growth!

Going to Eight in growth takes your best qualities and makes them accessible to others. Passion gives your ideas wings, and assertiveness gives you the confidence to speak up. Fives who are growing don't hide and hoard, nor are they paralyzed by laziness and gluttony. Fives who are growing see the value in their gifts and, with the Holy Spirit's help, share them for God's glory and our good.

Not only does going to Eight give you qualities you need, it also takes care of some of your pain points. All of these practiced skills help you with your propensity to hoard your time, talents, and so on, your analysis paralysis, and a myriad of other issues you may have when you're average to unhealthy.

Fives need the best qualities of Eight to be effective, just like Sevens need the best parts of Five to be effective. This is one of the gifts of learning about the Enneagram: seeing that what you need to grow is within arm's reach, that you are on a growth path thanks to the saving work of Jesus Christ, and that there are people out there who are strong where you are weak, and vice versa. We need each other. None of us is perfect just operating out of instincts and not pushing into growth.

SHIFT IN FOCUS

Do you struggle with confidence and asserting yourself? Both of these positive qualities are only positive when they come with a lot of communication, which can be difficult for some of us. We tend to believe that we can't impact our environment or the realities of our lives, even if we know deep down that is not true. We tend to sit back and let life happen, occasionally dodging bullets or refilling our iced tea.

But we know that God is a God of action, that obedience requires doing, and that a wasted life is just as sinful as a life lived in active sin.

Spend a moment in prayer asking God to convict you of the places where you are inactive, asking Him to give you the confidence to impact your realties for His glory and others' good.

● ● ● ● ● ● ● ● ● ● ● ● **DAY 53**

The Best of Type Eight

Be watchful, stand firm in the faith, act like men, be strong.
(1 Corinthians 16:13)

A healthy Eight is just as confident, energetic, and assertive as ever, but there's tangible compassion about the way they listen to and care for others. These Eights use their strength to protect the people in their lives in a way only an Eight can, and they often champion the underdogs in society.

Eights are the only Enneagram type that you can literally feel walk into a room. They are the football coach with confidence for days, the boss whose very presence inspires everyone to sit a little taller, and a friend who has the softest heart but everyone else finds intimidating.

There's a good reason why the Enneagram Eight is called the Challenger. With an energy and confidence about them that few can match, an Eight won't back away from a verbal spar. Eights can also be known as the Advocate because of their fire for justice. Wherever there's a protest against ill treatment, you'll probably find more than a handful of Eights shouting the loudest.

When Eights are healthy, they are great leaders, loyal friends, and a champion for anyone who can't stand up for themselves.

Type Eights are needed in a world where most of us would rather live unaffected and turn a blind eye to any problem that's not impacting us personally. We need Eights to light the fire and rally the troops.

I find that Eights and Fives are often drawn to each other as friends: they both appreciate the other for what they bring to the table, and often do this without judgment. You might find that the Eights in your life light a fire under you, and that's exactly what going to Eight in growth does. As a Five, you have many gifts and talents, but they aren't very effective if they are never put into action.

SHIFT IN FOCUS

Do you have any type Eights in your life?

What do you appreciate about them?

If applicable, during this next week, reach out and let the Eight in your life know how much you respect them. (This could even be a stranger on social media you know is an Eight.)

DAY 54

Why Fives Need Passion to Grow

His disciples remembered that it was written,
"Zeal for your house will consume me."
(John 2:17)

Passion means an intense feeling or longing toward something. We automatically know how different it feels if someone says they're *interested* in Korean culture versus saying they're *passionate* about Korean culture. Passion takes interest and knowledge and turns them into action.

Fives are masters at interest and knowledge, wanting to know something about everything. You're collectors of knowledge and sit with your toes in the water without ever actually jumping in. Passion is jumping in. Passion is getting in deep and taking risks. It's where your emotions and thoughts connect, and it's where thinking something meets doing something.

We don't forget our passions like we do our interests. Passion insinuates something that consumes you, something that you think a lot about—so much so that it impacts your actions.

We see an example of passion in John 2:13–17:

The Passover of the Jews was at hand, and Jesus went up to Jerusalem. In the temple he found those who were selling oxen and sheep and pigeons, and the money-changers sitting there. And making a whip of cords, he drove them all out of the temple, with the sheep and oxen. And he poured out the coins of the money-changers and overturned their tables.

And he told those who sold the pigeons, "Take these things away; do not make my Father's house a house of trade." His disciples remembered that it was written, "Zeal for your house will consume me."

Jesus's passion and love for His Father led Him to have a deep and zealous respect for His Father's house. When others were disrespecting this holy place by selling and trading, Jesus's passion prompted Him to action.

In your life, you may be interested in politics, but do you ever do anything that others can see? Are you on street corners with a sign, engaging with passersby? Do you talk to your family and friends about the importance of this topic to you? Do you act on the policies you claim are important to you? Are you willing to be the hands and feet of Christ?

As a Five, one of the most tempting sins in your life will always be inactivity, detachment, and being overprepared without actually doing anything. Doing the dirty work and saying something mean you might get hurt...or worse, exposed as being wrong. Passion will carry you where knowledge can't. You need passion because the temptation of inactivity is strong. You need passion because the world needs you to teach us with your actions, not just your thoughts.

SHIFT IN FOCUS

Can you clearly see the inactivity, detachment, and excessive preparation in your own life?

Where are the seeds of passion in your life, and how can you water them?

• • • • • • • • • • **DAY 55**

Growing in Assertiveness
By Anna Yates

*But I am like a green olive tree in the house of God. I trust in the
steadfast love of God forever and ever. I will thank you forever,
because you have done it. I will wait for your name, for it is good,
in the presence of the godly.*
(Psalm 52:8–9)

I was the kid who would break out in hives if I had to talk to
a stranger; nodding and one-word answers were my conversa-
tional tools. In high school, I got nervous simply ordering fast
food when my basketball team traveled to away games. I hated
talking to strangers on the phone. Each time I had to call to make
a doctor's appointment, I paced for half an hour trying to psych
myself into it.

When I discovered the Enneagram in college, learning I was
part of the relationist harmony triad helped me see how much I
did care about relationships. I see the world in terms of interper-
sonal connections, and I realized that a lot of my fear was rooted
in feeling unsafe and incapable, feeling rejected before I'd even
gotten into a situation.

All of the *lone wolf* bravado I'd built up to protect myself
was just a facade. Deep down, the core of my desire for competence and fear of making an idiot of myself was a desire to be connected. I was hiding behind competence to try to make myself
feel safe in an overwhelming world.

Dear Five, *you* are safe, even when you don't feel like it.

The deeper I go with God, the more unknowns He leads me to, and the more trust He calls me to. In the past several years, I've experienced a few false starts in the career department, a messy but beautiful romance, a solid job that paid well but wasn't in a healthy environment, a calling to start a new business and jump in full time, and many more situations. Regardless of how I feel in any given moment, "*I am like a green olive tree in the house of God*"—nurtured and flourishing because I trust in God's unfailing love.

My growth path to assertiveness has been the opposite of natural or logical. I've had to let go of the need to protect myself, trusting that God has the answers, energy, and resources I need.

Growing in assertiveness and moving toward Eight is really all about speaking up and stepping out, moving from the mental realm where we're so comfortable as Fives and into the scary realm of action, risks, and trust. The more we trust that we're safe, the more we can speak up about our needs, feelings, and experiences, and step out to experience the world instead of forever observing it.

SHIFT IN FOCUS

Are you weary, dear Five? Jesus has the rest and strength that's perfect for you in this moment.

Are you confused? Jesus knows the big picture, even if you don't get to see it right now.

Are you hurting? Jesus is with you in this breath and desires to draw you closer to heal you.

Let His presence breathe peace into your mind.

Let His acceptance flow into the dry places of your heart, giving life.

Let His courage embolden your body to healthy, productive action.

You are safe because He's got you.

DAY 56 • • • • • • • • • •

Growing in Boundaries
By Jarrett Bradley

But he turned and said to Peter, "Get behind me, Satan! You are a hindrance to me. For you are not setting your mind on the things of God, but on the things of man."
(Matthew 16:23)

Rather, speaking the truth in love, we are to grow up in every way into him who is the head, into Christ.
(Ephesians 4:15)

Growing in boundaries can be one of the most helpful tools for doing life well. Boundaries are fundamentally about defining what you are responsible for…and what you are *not* responsible for. Having boundaries allows for both freedom and focus: freedom from taking on things that are not, in fact, ours to take on, either physically or emotionally; and focus by limiting or eliminating unnecessary experiences so that we have more energy for the things we actually value.

Doing boundaries well, however, is no easy feat and takes practice, patience, and assertiveness. Boundaries always begin with determining what is actually your responsibility, and that step alone can take time to ascertain. This can be especially true in environments where ingrained patterns of functioning have been established, like in families or workplaces. These areas are usually the hardest places to enforce new boundaries because there are long-time expectations that relationships will continue the ways they always have.

Jesus was a master at keeping good boundaries with those around Him, not only with the government and religious elite, but also His most intimate friends. Consider this: as God Himself, the source of love, Jesus was the most loving human who has ever lived. It thus seems surprising for Him to state—to His *good friend* Peter—"*Get behind me, Satan!*" So, was Jesus being nasty to Peter in this moment? No. In fact, it was quite the opposite. Jesus was establishing a boundary with Peter in the only way Peter would be sure to hear, and doing so was the most loving thing possible for both Peter and Jesus Himself.

The always-bold Peter was rebuking Jesus for stating that He would die, so Jesus came back strong. Peter had expectations for who and what the Christ would be and how He would rise to power. However, these things were not in Peter's control, and they were not his responsibility. So when he tried to bend Jesus to fit his mold, Jesus immediately set him straight in the only way Peter would hear.

We too are called to have good boundaries with those around us, especially those we are closest to. It can be difficult to enforce boundaries, but the burden of asserting them is made considerably lighter when we recognize that clearly communicated limits are loving for all parties, even if one of them thinks otherwise. It is cruel to let others think they have the power to unload their responsibilities onto us—or try to lay them on anyone else for that matter—and we love them by establishing what we can and cannot take on.

As a practical word of advice: if someone comes to you and asks you to do something you are unsure you should be doing, you can always say, "I'll think about it and get back to you." But if they need an answer *now*, then the answer is no.

SHIFT IN FOCUS

Can you think of any areas in your life where others ask you to take responsibility for things that they are responsible for?

Are you ever made to feel guilty if you don't do things for other people, especially with your family or at work?

What would it take to see establishing boundaries with those individuals as loving?

• • • • • • • • • • • DAY 57

Growing in Engagement
By Anna Yates

For this reason I remind you to fan into flame the gift of God,
which is in you through the laying on of my hands, for God gave
us a spirit not of fear but of power and love and self-control.
(2 Timothy 1:6–7)

One of the telltale signs that convinced me I'm a Five is that I get anxious when I have to jump into an activity when I don't feel like I've had enough time to prepare. As a child and teenager, I would stand to the side in new social situations, environments, or games in order to observe. Once I figured out the situation, I'd start making friends, moving where I needed to go, and participating. Withdrawal and overthinking are my go-to coping mechanisms.

A few years ago, I found out about a dance studio that offered group classes, and I decided to try it out. During one salsa class, the instructor kept telling me I needed to loosen up and press into my partner's hand so I could feel the way he was leading. He said, "You don't have to know all the steps. You just have to press in and follow your partner's lead." As the class continued and we rotated partners down the line, I still struggled to figure out the steps instead of letting my partner lead me. Finally, one of my dancing partners sensed my tension and said, "It's alright; I've got you."

That night was a revelation for me. The dance was a physical metaphor for showing up, letting go of control, and trusting that God's got me. Just like I don't have to know all the salsa steps, I'm not going to understand everything about what God's doing right now. And I don't have to. All I have to do is show up, press in, and follow the lead.

Dear Five, *God's got you.*

Withdrawal is my coping mechanism, but it often leaves me confused and alone. I've found the more I try to figure things out so that I'll act appropriately and confidently, the more insecure I feel. The more I withdraw, the more I feel the need to withdraw. The less I trust, the more my fears come true.

At its core, the need to understand is the need to be safe. The more I accept that I am safe because God's got me, the more I can relax and show up where God's calling me. I can speak up about my needs and my feelings instead of hiding in fear because God's got me. I can step out in the good ideas God's given me, even when they're not fully planned or perfect, instead of questioning myself and gathering more knowledge. God's got me.

SHIFT IN FOCUS

Read 2 Timothy 1, paying special attention to verses 5–14.

If these words reflect your heart, please borrow them:

Dear heavenly Father, I release the tension inside my mind, heart, and body. I choose to stop standing on the sidelines and waiting for "enough." I accept that You've got me, and You make me safe. I let go and let You sweep me up in the beautiful rhythm of life with You. Even though it's scary, I pursue intimacy with You. I trust You. Amen.

DAY 58 • • • • • • • • • • •

Growing in Using Your Talents
By Anna Yates

*He also who had received the one talent came forward, saying,
"Master, I knew you to be a hard man, reaping where you did not
sow, and gathering where you scattered no seed, so I was afraid,
and I went and hid your talent in the ground. Here, you have what
is yours." But his master answered him, "You wicked and slothful
servant! You knew that I reap where I have not sown and gather
where I scattered no seed? Then you ought to have invested my
money with the bankers, and at my coming I should have received
what was my own with interest."*
(Matthew 25:24–27)

In college, I read a book that captured my imagination. Reading
it was like a movie reel playing in my mind. I couldn't shake the
idea of adapting this story into a play.

As a nineteen-year-old who didn't have a live-and-breathe
background in theater, that seemed like a bite too big to chew.
When I tried to talk about the idea, the words choked in my
throat. But as I prayed, I felt God giving me a vision for the play
to be a community experience, something that wasn't just enter-
taining but brought attention to important issues and the orga-
nizations solving them.

I started sharing the idea more, and it gained momentum.
Over two years of collaboration and hard work, I adapted, pro-
duced, and directed the play with an amazing cast, crew, and

audience response. It was an impactful experience for everyone, and the insights and friendships God gave me through it are so precious.

So, fellow Five, what's that idea that keeps nagging at you, the passion that makes your heart race, the skill you're really good at, the thing you feel so at home with?

Dear Five, your voice, your ideas, and your heart should not be hidden treasures.

The parable of the talents makes it clear what happens when we reject or hide what God gives us. The talents represent investments, things of value that the master entrusted to his servants to multiply his holdings. When one steward buried his treasure, the master was rightfully angry and punished him.

I've always understood how the last steward must have felt: he was so afraid that he would fail that he did nothing with that talent. He was afraid that whatever he did wouldn't be enough and he would be rejected even if he tried. He doubted that his ideas, voice, or actions were actually special or important.

Deep down, the servant who buried the talent entrusted to him had a trust issue.

But God doesn't give us leftover gifts. He uses what He gives us and wants us to use our gifts too. Often, all it takes is being brave enough to show up, step out, and take the action that terrifies us. When God invests in us by giving us a godly desire, good idea, or resource, He just asks us to step out in faith and trust Him for the rest. The closer I am to Him, the more He shines through my every move, and the more He multiplies my efforts for His kingdom. Remember, we have more to lose by hiding than we do by showing up.

SHIFT IN FOCUS

What investments has God made in you?

What are ways God has already used these investments to spread goodness?

Where can you show up and give even more with those investments?

If these words reflect your heart, please borrow them:

Dear heavenly Father, I see the investments You've put inside me. I recognize my fear of opening up and using my passions, voice, heart, and resources to their full extent. I unburden myself to You about all of the hurt and rejection I've felt around these things. I relinquish control over them. I'm available to You. Use me to benefit Your kingdom. Amen.

• • • • • • • • • • • **DAY 59**

The Passionate Five

And let us not grow weary of doing good, for in due season we will
reap, if we do not give up.
(Galatians 6:9)

Do a quick Google search of "people who have changed the world."

Although we can't know these people's Enneagram numbers for sure, we see a lot of themes that feel Eight-ish and Five-ish. We have the crusaders, military officials, and fighters—people who changed the world with their hands: Eights. And we find the engineers, philosophers, and inventors—people who changed the world with their minds: Fives.

Although any type can change the world, using your hands or mind to do so feels distinctly Eight-ish and Five-ish. Eights and Fives share a vein of passion that doesn't let them live peacefully and die.

When Fives grow in Eight-ness, they can have a positive impact on the people with whom they interact. You might not even know how you are helping others in your lifetime, but with our big God and your big passion, you can do a lot of good in your short time here on earth.

Now, going to Eight in growth doesn't just magically happen; it will involve some work on your part. But seasons of growth will make these skills easier to access. So if you recognize a growth season, prioritize practicing Eight-ish skills. Your growth might look a lot like action and choosing to do the uncomfortable work of growth, knowing that our adversary, the devil, doesn't want you to grow in Christ or change the world for the good.

SHIFT IN FOCUS

Which person from your Google search stood out to you the most?

What did you learn that you didn't know before?

Invite God to convict you to act and be bold where you wouldn't naturally be inclined to be.

• • • • • • • • • • • DAY 60

The Risk-Taking Five

Practice these things, immerse yourself in them,
so that all may see your progress.
(1 Timothy 4:15)

At first, prioritizing growth may not feel like accomplishing much; in fact, it may feel like giving up. Every moment you are convicted to rest or trust and don't, the reality of growth becomes further and further from the reality in your head. Again and again, you may fail to take action on prioritizing these things because it just feels too hard, and then you'll feel beaten down and not enough. This is the challenge of being motivated by competency and wanting to grow but being afraid of that steep learning curve. What if you look like a fool in the process? What if you say the wrong thing? What if your passion is fleeting and you're acting recklessly? These feelings are something Satan uses to make sure you never walk in the freedom of your worth in Christ.

Satan is all about stopping your growth from coming to fruition. I wouldn't be surprised if you even notice elements of spiritual attack as you prioritize growth. But that doesn't mean the growth isn't God's heart for you.

Going to Eight in growth will feel painful at times, and you'll get discouraged. Remember that life is seasonal and you will not achieve your ultimate state of growth here on earth. You cannot become your ideal self because you will never be without a sinful nature while you're still breathing here. However, this doesn't mean that you are not growing. By the power of the Holy Spirit, you are in the process of a beautiful becoming.

Don't let two steps forward and one step back discourage you. This is still moving forward; this is still growing.

Passion, action, and asserting yourself may feel scary at times because you're trusting God for the outcome. You're trusting that peace is better than the satisfaction of being in control. You're trusting the truth that God is the God of hope, and that hope is something He wants for you. Like the child at the edge of the pool jumping into their father's arms, you're trusting that God is ready to catch you.

SHIFT IN FOCUS

Here, we are going to use 1 Timothy 4:15 as a guideline for action:

Practice these things, immerse yourself in them, so that all may see your progress.

"Practice these things"

Every new thing you've ever done needed some practicing. Growing in going to Eight is no different. Practice by asserting yourself, plan for things that fill you with passion, and choose one action that can be your next right thing. Every small step counts.

"Immerse yourself in them"

What verse that we mentioned over the last ten days really stuck out to you? I would encourage you to memorize it, write it out, and place it somewhere you will see it. Immerse yourself in the truth of your worth in Christ, and you'll find yourself slowly but surely believing it to be true.

"So that all may see your progress"

Pick a couple of people in your life to share your big or small victories with. I hope you have a couple of people come to mind right away, but if not, there are plenty of Instagram or Facebook pages for Fives with followers who would love to cheer you on in your Five-ish wins. Be bold and share them as something worth celebrating. Go get yourself a coffee, or have a bowl of ice cream! Life is hard, and any victories are worth celebrating with God and others.

BOOK RECOMMENDATIONS FOR FIVES

Greg McKeown, *Essentialism: The Disciplined Pursuit of Less* (New York: Currency, 2014)

Dallas Willard, *The Divine Conspiracy: Rediscovering Our Hidden Life in God* (San Francisco: Harper, 1998)

John Ortberg, *Soul Keeping: Caring for the Most Important Part of You* (Grand Rapids, MI: Zondervan, 2014)

Emily P. Freeman, *The Next Right Thing: A Simple, Soulful Practice for Making Life Decisions* (Grand Rapids, MI: Revell, 2019)

Leeana Tankersley, *Begin Again: The Brave Practice of Releasing Hurt & Receiving Rest* (Grand Rapids, MI: Revell, 2018)

Susan Cain, *Quiet: The Power of Introverts in a World That Can't Stop Talking* (New York: Crown Publishers, 2012)

Hannah Anderson, *All That's Good: Recovering the Lost Art of Discernment* (Chicago: Moody Publishers, 2018)

Jamie C. Martin, *Introverted Mom: Your Guide to More Calm, Less Guilt, and Quiet Joy* (Grand Rapids, MI: Zondervan, 2019)

As the Enneagram has passed through many hands, and been taught by various wonderful people, I want to acknowledge that none of the concepts or ideas of the Enneagram have been created by me. I'd like to give thanks to the Enneagram teachers and pioneers who have gone before me, and whose work has influenced this devotional:

Suzanne Stabile

Ian Morgan Cron

Father Richard Rohr

Don Richard Riso

Russ Hudson

Beatrice Chestnut

Beth McCord

Ginger Lapid-Bogda

ABOUT THE AUTHOR

Elisabeth Bennett first discovered the Enneagram in the summer of 2017 and immediately realized how life-changing this tool could be. She set out to absorb all she could about this ancient personality typology, including a twelve-week Enneagram Certification course taught by Beth McCord, who has studied the Enneagram for more than twenty-five years.

Elisabeth quickly started her own Enneagram Instagram account (@Enneagram.Life), which has grown to more than 70,000 followers. Since becoming a certified Enneagram coach, Elisabeth has conducted more than three hundred one-on-one coaching sessions focused on helping her clients find their type and apply the Enneagram to their lives for personal and spiritual growth. She has also conducted staff/team building sessions for businesses and high school students.

Elisabeth has lived in beautiful Washington State her entire life and now has the joy of raising her own children there with her husband, Peter.

To contact Elisabeth, please visit:

www.elisabethbennettenneagram.com

www.instagram.com/enneagram.life

Welcome to Our House!

We Have a Special Gift for You

It is our privilege and pleasure to share in your love of Christian books. We are committed to bringing you authors and books that feed, challenge, and enrich your faith.

To show our appreciation, we invite you to sign up to receive a specially selected **Reader Appreciation Gift**, with our compliments. Just go to the Web address at the bottom of this page.

God bless you as you seek a deeper walk with Him!

WE HAVE A GIFT FOR YOU. VISIT:

whpub.me/nonfictionthx

WHITAKER
HOUSE

1 · GOODNESS · TRUTH · PERFECTION · CLARITY · JUSTICE · SELF CONTROL ·

2 · HELPFULNESS · ALTRUISM · LOVING · BOLD · SERVANTS HEART · DISCERNING NEEDS ·

3 · EFFICIENCY · ACTION · ENCOURAGER · ESTABLISHER · INSPIRING · EXCELLENCE ·

4 · CREATIVITY · EMPATHY · LOVE OF BEAUTY · SPACE SAVER · EMOTIONALLY HONEST ·

5 · WISDOM · VISION · STEADFASTNESS · CLARITY · FAITHFULNESS · HUMILITY ·

6 · COURAGE · GUARDIANSHIP · KINDNESS · LOYALTY · STRENGTH · FAITHFULNESS ·

7 · SPONTANEITY · JOY · THANKFULNESS · HOPE · LONG SUFFERING · VISION ·

8 · STRENGTH · ZEAL · VIGILANT · JUSTICE · PROTECTOR · TENDERNESS ·

9 · PEACE · KINDNESS · EMPATHY · PATIENCE · GENTLENESS · UNDERSTANDING ·

STRESS

① ② ③ ④ ⑤ ⑥ ⑦ ⑧ ⑨